FIRST SENTENCES
— for —
Network Marketing

How To
Quickly Get Prospects
On Your Side

TOM "BIG AL" SCHREITER

For information, contact:

Fortune Network Publishing
PO Box 890084
Houston, TX 77289 USA

Telephone: +1 (281) 280-9800

ISBN: 1-892366-37-1

ISBN-13: 978-1-892366-37-5

DEDICATION

This book is dedicated to network marketers everywhere.

I travel the world 240+ days each year. Let me know if you want me to stop in your area and conduct a live Big Al training.

http://www.BigAlSeminars.com

Get 7 mini-reports of amazing, easy sentences that create new, hot prospects.

Sign up today at:

http://www.BigAlReport.com

Other great Big Al Books available at:

http://www.BigAlBooks.com

TABLE OF CONTENTS

PREFACE

We decide to eat at a restaurant, frequently before we have even seen the menu. And we judge a video on the first few seconds.

Why?

Because we are busy. We try to avoid time-wasting activities such as listening to long, boring sales presentations. Our minds instantly decide if we like the salesman, or not. Our minds instantly decide if the salesman's offer will be interesting to us, or not.

And finally, our minds instantly decide if we should trust and believe the salesman.

We make these decisions based upon the first sentence, or the first few sentences. We are only seconds away from success ... or failure.

If our first sentences are bad, it is over. We don't have a chance.

Want to improve your business? The fastest way is to improve your first sentence.

— Tom "Big Al" Schreiter

Distributors aren't lazy.

Lazy people don't skip their favorite cable television shows to attend an opportunity meeting. Lazy people don't invest in an expensive distributor kit, promotional literature and products. And lazy people don't commit part-time hours every week to build a future for themselves and their families.

So why are my distributors not working?

New distributors have two problems.

1. They don't know what to do.

2. They do the wrong things.

These are serious problems.

I conduct trainings throughout the world. During the first hour of my Super Sponsoring Workshops, I ask the attendees a simple question:

"What is the **first** sentence out of your mouth when you make a business presentation to a prospect?"

The silence is uncomfortable.

The attendees **avoid** eye contact.

The attendees pretend to look at their notes.

The whole room squirms in agony, hoping that someone, anyone, will answer that question. If I didn't say anything, nothing more would happen for the rest of the day!

Finally I give the attendees some relief. I explain that we only have **one chance** to make a good first impression. If our first impression is great, we can make mistakes for the rest of our presentation and our prospect will still like us ... and still want to join.

If our first impression causes our prospect to put up his defenses, mentally guard his wallet, and evaluate every future statement from a negative, skeptical mindset, then we are in big trouble. We could give the best presentation, complete with a laser light show, and **the prospect still wouldn't join**.

That's how important our first sentence is in our presentation. It's almost everything.

This holds true for any presentation:

* an opportunity meeting,

* a prospecting telephone call,

* or a business presentation across the kitchen table.

Your first sentence will determine the mood and cooperation of your prospect.

A bad first sentence will cause your prospect to fold his arms, put up his defenses, guard his wallet, and listen with a skeptical attitude.

A great first sentence will make your prospect a partner. Your prospect will forgive the fact that you can't remember the name of your company, that you get confused on the product ingredients, and that you don't have a clue how the compensation plan works.

Your prospect makes decisions in the first few seconds such as:

* "Should I trust this person?"

* "Should I believe what this person says?"

* "Do I like this person?"

* "Is this person trying to take advantage of me?"

* "Do I want to do business with this person?"

This is why we must develop a great first sentence. Most trainings concentrate on how to present the products or compensation plan. Hours and hours are spent memorizing and practicing presentation and closing techniques.

That is wasted effort!

If the opening sentence is great, you can mangle the rest of your presentation and prospects will still beg you to let them join. Or, at the very least, prospects will give you a fair hearing.

Think of it this way:

"I would rather have my distributors give lousy presentations to prospects who love them, than give great presentations to prospects who hate them."

So, back to the Super Sponsoring Workshop and the uncomfortable attendees. I have asked the attendees to tell me the first sentence out of their mouth when they give a presentation.

And then the excuses begin.

The attendees say:

* "Oh, I just kind of think something up, whatever feels good at the moment."

* "I always start with the second sentence. I never use a first sentence."

* "I'm confused. Do you mean the first sentence at an opportunity meeting? Or do you mean the first sentence at an in-home presentation?"

* "I just wing it."

* "It depends on the prospect, the weather, or how I feel."

* "I concentrate on a multimedia presentation of the compensation plan. I never worry about how the prospect feels."

Right. Sure.

Want to know what the attendees are **really** saying? They are saying:

"I don't know what to say."

Their sponsors **never taught them** the importance and strategy of a good first sentence. They were never taught effective first words to say to start a successful business presentation. That is sad.

When your distributors:

1. Don't know what to do,

2. Don't know exactly what to say,

3. And don't know how to start a successful presentation,

Guess what?

They don't do anything!

Distributors aren't lazy.

They desperately want to build a business.

They just don't know what to say and do.

You only get one chance to make a good first impression. Yet, untrained distributors destroy good prospects and turn them into bloody clumps of anti-networking vigilantes.

Here is a test.

Write down the first sentence out of your mouth when you give a business presentation to a prospect.

* Does your first sentence turn the prospect off?

* Does your first sentence make you sound like a salesman?

* Does your first sentence make the prospect put up sales-resistant shields?

Or does your first sentence make your prospect immediately want to be your partner?

Just pause now for a minute. Write down, or say out loud, the first sentence you use.

A simple sentence to get your prospect's instant attention.

Before starting your presentation, you could say:

* "If you have a few minutes, I would like to tell you how you can quit your job and still make more money."

* "If you have a few minutes, I would like to tell you how you can get a full-time income by working two nights a week."

* "If you have a few minutes, I would like to tell you how you can get a new car and never have to make car payments again."

* "If you have a few minutes, I would like to tell you how we can become millionaires."

* "If you have a few minutes, I would like to tell you how we can get free vacations for life."

* "If you have a few minutes, I would like to tell you how my friend got a 50% raise, and now works from home."

* "If you have a few minutes, I would like to tell you how we can be in business together."

* "If you have a few minutes, I would like to tell you how I get business tax deductions, just like the big companies."

"If you have a few minutes ..." is a great opening phrase that is polite and avoids rejection.

Isn't that more interesting?

Those are examples of first sentences that may interest your prospect.

Here are some examples of first sentences that may create sales alarms and resistance in your prospects:

* "Let me tell you about my wonderful business."

* "I've got a great opportunity that I know would be perfect for you."

* "Do you keep your residual income options open?"

* "I just got involved with the most wonderful company and products ..."

* "This is a ground-floor opportunity guaranteed to be a winner."

Well, you get the idea.

Some sentences will create good, open-minded prospects who are willing to listen to us, and some sentences will close the minds of our prospects instantly.

Use your imagination.

Pretend you are the prospect. What would the prospect like to hear?

For example, if you want an opening question to prime your prospects on the power of the tax advantages of a home-based business, try some of **my favorites** such as:

* "Would you like to get a $100 tax refund every month?"

* "Are you paying the maximum taxes allowed by law by being a job holder?"

* "Would you like to get some of the tax deductions used by the wealthy?"

* "Would you like to celebrate April 15th every year - and laugh while your friends pay taxes?" (April 15th is tax day in the U.S.)

Ideas?

And finally, here are some of my favorite headlines and first sentences to kickstart your imagination before we start the next chapter:

"Is this your secret problem?" (Curiosity makes this one easy.)

"Skip commuting and work from your home." (The pain of sitting in traffic and burning expensive fuel will motivate this prospect to listen.)

"99% of your friends are wrong." (Since we agree, we want to hear more.)

"Take 3 inches off your waistline this weekend." (As dieters, we will hold out eternal hope for almost any dieting promise. The next few examples demonstrate that promise to dieters.)

"The fat-burner that works while you sleep."

"The herbal diet remedy that almost works too quickly."

"Only dumb people diet the old-fashioned way."

"Do you know anyone with Christmas bills?" (Very specific target statement. If we know someone with this problem, then we will have their total attention.)

"How to change a dead-end career." (Attracts someone who is open-minded and has not given up hope.)

"When NOT to eat healthy." (Got my attention right away!)

"Three reasons to fire your boss tomorrow." (Gives prospects a vision of changing their lives immediately.)

"How to get rid of debt in just three years." (Three years seems realistic and believable.)

"Why your neighbors and friends get ahead - and you don't!" (We all think that others have some secret that we don't know. We have to know more!)

"Never pay a mobile phone bill again." (People get excited because they feel overcharged by utility providers.)

"Only three hours of sleep - here's proof!" (I learned this from Art Jonak. If you add the words "Here's proof!" ... people are naturally curious to know more.)

"Take a six-month vacation twice a year and hire your boss to do the work." (Totally unrealistic, but we dream, and want to hear more.)

"Think like a millionaire." (Thinking doesn't sound too hard. Seems like an easy step to take.)

"Why this 28-year-old high school dropout earns more than his boss." (We feel that we have more skills and more knowledge than a 28-year-old dropout. Gives us confidence that we can surpass the dropout's results.)

"Look like a millionaire for less than $50." (Doesn't sound hard. Who wouldn't want to look awesome for less than $50?)

"Earn more money than your spouse can spend." (The humor will bring a smile to the prospect's face, and will naturally lower the sales resistance.)

"Have that exclusive spa facial look for only $1.95 a day." (Reducing the cost to a daily amount is an easy way to get past price resistance.)

"Do you swallow hard when your boss tells you to work overtime?" (We all have pride and hate feeling powerless. This question strikes hard at those emotions.)

"Retire at age 35 - not age 65." (And you could change that age to 25 if you were talking to younger prospects.)

"Kiss your credit card debt goodbye." (Targets people who have crushing minimum payments on their credit cards. Their motivation for more money to make these payments will keep their minds open for your presentation.)

"Kiss your mortgage goodbye." (People dream of the extra cash flow when they don't have huge mortgage payments.)

"Let strokes and heart attacks happen to somebody else." (To live forever ... yes! Or at least a long time. It is the unknown that stresses prospects. Here is a promise to remove this unknown and relieve them of that stress.)

Two really short first sentences.

Prepare two envelopes.

On the outside of one envelope, write the word:

"Interested."

On the outside of the other envelope, write the words:

"Not Interested."

First sentences don't get much shorter than that.

Now, approach a prospect with your two envelopes and have a short conversation.

If the prospect is not interested in attending an opportunity meeting, hearing about your business or product, or reviewing a pre-approach package, look at your two envelopes and give him the envelope marked, "Not Interested."

The prospect will notice your other envelope marked, "Interested." The curiosity begins. Your prospect might be thinking, "Hey, I really want to know what is in the 'Interested' envelope. Maybe I should change my mind and be interested. Maybe I should ask for a presentation."

If the prospect is truly not interested, he will receive the envelope marked "Not Interested" and can review the contents of the "Not Interested" envelope at his leisure. You can place some discounted coupons for your product or service in this envelope, or maybe put in a letter asking for referrals.

What can you put into the "Interested" envelope?

Use your imagination.

You could have an application, a catalog, testimonials, a getting-started audio or coupons for free training. The point of the exercise is that most prospects want what is inside the "Interested" envelope.

You see, first sentences don't have to be long. They could be as little as one or two words.

Prospects have short attention spans, but will respond if our first sentences and headlines have clear benefits.

Some short first sentences and headline ideas?

* "The 15-second diet."

* "Jobless."

* "Turbo training day."

* "Keep your taxes."

* "Tax relief in one hour."

* "Quit your job at full pay."

* "24-hour energy drink."

* "Free mobile service."

* "Sugar-free munchie bar."

* "One-calorie super-vitamin program."

* "Overnight youth."

* "Instant discount."

* "Awesome health in a capsule."

* "Lose 2 pounds a week."

* "Cash for shopping."

* "No more wrinkles."

* "Fire your boss."

* "3-day weekends forever."

* "Foot-high pies." (I personally tried four of these pies, but they only averaged 10 inches high. Still, I wasn't disappointed.)

Because these are very short first sentences and headlines, they are perfect for car signs and other limited-space advertising. All of these examples leave plenty of room for your telephone number or website.

Each of these first sentences makes a powerful opening statement. Perfect for networking events and speeches, too.

What about the telephone?

The telephone is intimidating for new distributors who don't know what to say. New distributors instinctively know that their first sentence might doom them, and they are afraid of saying the wrong thing.

What can I say for an opening sentence when dealing with telephone inquiries?

Many times it is not so much **what** you say, but **how** you say it.

For example, let's say that we have a magic phrase that works wonderfully. We say:

"I would like to show you how you can build a nice part-time income."

This statement may work for some distributors, but not for others. Why?

Because of **who** you are ... and what you **believe**.

Suppose a sleazy used car salesman said,

"I would like to show you how you can build a nice part-time income."

It wouldn't be too effective, would it?

Suppose a three-year-old child said,

"I would like to show you how you can build a nice part-time income."

The prospect wouldn't respond favorably, even though the right words were said. The prospect would be thinking that the three-year-old child doesn't have credibility.

What happens when you believe what you are saying?

If you truly believe that you can help the person calling, it comes through in your voice. The prospect instinctively **feels** who you are and what you believe in. And that feeling is more important than the actual words you use.

Now, for a few ideas on what you could say:

* "Thanks for calling. Which part of the ad interested you?"

* "Thanks for calling. What would you like me to tell you first?"

* "Thanks for calling. What type of opportunity are you looking for?"

All of these statements are simple. Remember, there is no magic in the above sentences. The magic is not in **what** you say, but **how** you say it.

Jackie's solution.

I was in San Antonio, Texas, talking with Jackie Clayton. I asked Jackie what made the difference when she is calling leads.

When the prospect answers the phone, she says:

"I see you have been looking for a home-based business. So why haven't you found a home business yet?"

Then Jackie explained why these two sentences work so well.

"The key is the question: 'So why haven't you found a home business yet?'"

Jackie continued: "The prospects relax, they do the talking, I do the listening. They tell me exactly why they didn't choose other businesses and now I know exactly what they are looking for. So when I then tell them about my business, it's easy."

I thought about this approach and it makes sense.

First, your prospects feel good because they can talk instead of us doing all the talking and selling.

Second, if you listen closely, then you will know how to approach these prospects in a way that will make it easier for them to accept your information.

And **third**, this is an almost rejection-free way of having a conversation with prospects. This should make cold-call recruiting much more pleasant.

Need a few more first sentence and headline ideas? Try these.

* "Tavern philosopher finally earns real money in his new business."

* "Four reasons your career is hazardous to your bank account."

* "Former fatmaster reveals his no-exercise weight-loss secret."

* "How two uninspired couch potatoes now receive weekly paychecks in their mailboxes."

* "How a personality-enriched accountant shows ordinary people how to start a new business."

* "Knoxville housewife helps office workers break the job habit."

* "How this herbal fat-burner will take three inches off your waistline in just seven days."

* "Why an overpaid bank officer quit his job to earn more money for his family."

* "49-year-old former caddy starts his own part-time business, and now owns his own golf course."

Facts tell. Stories sell.

Almost 40 years ago, I wrote a book about sponsoring. In the book, I told my readers that:

"Facts tell. Stories sell."

That explanation was too short to be useful for most readers. I am sure that most readers read the two sentences, smiled, and then quickly moved on to the next chapter.

Recently I attended a workshop.

I was listening to the speakers explain why stories sell and facts only tell. I listened with interest, not only because what they were saying was true, but they also had the results to prove it. Their businesses were growing rapidly.

Here is what really caught my attention.

Their first sentence!

They did the following demonstration. To the first person in the audience, they said:

"I have a wonderful business opportunity. Would you like to hear about it?"

Of course the prospect said that he was not interested, too busy, and just leaving to make an important phone call.

Most people are not interested in the **fact** that you have a wonderful business opportunity.

To the second person in the audience, they said:

"Let me tell you what happened to me just two days ago."

The second person replied, "What happened?"

The speakers were then able to start a business presentation.

Because the prospect assumed it was a **story** - the prospect wanted to know how the story ended. Everyone is interested in how a story ends. That is why soap operas are so popular on television.

If you don't see the profound difference in these two approaches, you are missing something really big.

Your distributors **hate** rejection. And to avoid rejection, they will not contact people.

The second approach, which is telling a prospect a story, **prevents rejection**. This almost guarantees that a presentation gets started with some positive momentum.

And if you don't know how to start a story, just say these words:

"I've got a good story."

These words are hard to resist.

People like stories about people.

People are interested in other people. It is in our nature.

So let's make our first sentences and offers about people, not facts.

This is a huge lesson for us to use in our business. This should change how we introduce our opportunity, our service, or our products.

Want some examples?

Which first sentence do you find more interesting and effective?

A. Our opportunity provides you with built-in tax advantages that can reduce your effective tax rate from 31% to 28%.

B. Let me tell you about the lady from Fairfield, Vermont who now earns an extra $350 a week and can stay home with her children.

Hmmm. Not a tough choice, is it? Most people want to hear about the lady from Fairfield.

A. Our "Super Product" has 15 more milligrams of Omega Fatty Acids than the store brand at Mega-Mart.

B. Let me tell you how Michelle lost two inches off her waistline by taking our "Super Product" for only three days.

Okay, this one isn't very hard either. We want to know more about Michelle.

A. Our mobile telephone can be used anywhere in the world, and it is easy to make calls.

B. Thank goodness John and Mary had our mobile calling plan when their daughter failed to get on that flight from Portland ...

Yes, "B" is more interesting because "B" is about people. We are programmed to be interested in people.

So the big lesson is easy. Talk about people ... and prospects will listen.

If your prospects aren't listening, you might want to change your first sentence. Don't blame the prospects. Blame the person saying the first sentence.

My favorite first sentence.

How do you overcome the fear of talking to prospects, even when your opportunity and products are great?

There are a lot of reasons for this fear. Here is one of the biggest reasons.

We feel that our opening sentence will cause prospects to think we are a salesman trying to take advantage of them. This is especially true with relatives and friends. We don't want to appear to be taking advantage of our friendship.

This is why the opening sentence is so important ... it sets the stage or mood for the entire presentation. Have you ever had a good opening, and everything went smoothly after that?

So what is my favorite first sentence?

I have been using this first sentence for over 20 years. It is not right for every situation, but when the situation is right, it completely pre-sells our prospects.

"Most people do network marketing every day, but they just don't get paid for it."

You might be wondering:

"Why does Big Al keep saying this same phrase over and over again?"

Because not only does this sentence pre-sell the prospect, it also strengthens the belief in new distributors every time they say it.

New distributors discover how easy this business can be. Prospects are already doing this business every day.

If your new distributor masters this sentence, then the rest of the conversations with prospects are easy.

As usual, I will use a story to help my new distributor remember this principle. Here it is.

The story.

Network marketing is **recommending** and **promoting** the things you like to other people.

We networkers, and most everyone else, do this activity almost every day. Networking is a natural skill that everyone **already** has! In network marketing, we simply collect residual income checks for doing what we do every day.

How about an example of daily networking?

Let's go to the mall.

I take my newest distributor to the local shopping mall to buy some shoes. After looking at many wonderful shoes in the store, she says, "Oh, I don't know. They all look sort of nice. But, it really depends on the purse."

Purse? I thought we were shopping for shoes. I didn't know you aren't allowed to buy shoes unless they match a purse.

I don't want this shoe-shopping experience to last forever, so I ask the shoe salesperson, "Where is a good store to look at purses here in the shopping mall?"

She replies, "Oh, there are many good purse stores, but the one by the food court with the brown purse over the door ... it is awesome. I go there during my breaks. It is a purse-buyer's wonderland."

Okay. My new distributor and I are off to the purse store, based upon the recommendation of the shoe salesperson.

And the shoe salesperson was right. This is an awesome purse store. We spend 45 minutes just looking at the off-brown single strap purse collection. And of course, my new distributor hasn't chosen a purse yet.

Because I am getting hungry, I ask, "Why haven't you chosen a purse yet?"

My new distributor replies, "You just can't pick a purse. You have to consider the clothes you will be wearing. The purse shouldn't clash with the clothes."

Desperate for food, I ask the purse salesperson, "Which store has the fastest selection of businesswear for women?"

The purse salesperson replies, "Fastest?"

"Yes. I am in a hurry. I am getting hungry, too."

The purse salesperson quickly recommends the business suit outlet store at the other end of the shopping mall. So, we are off to look at business clothing based upon the purse salesperson's recommendation and promotion.

We pass the food court as my new distributor is focused on nice business clothes that don't clash with a purse, and making sure that the purse matches the shoes she hasn't bought yet.

Of course you know what happens at the businesswear outlet. No clothes can be purchased unless they can be accessorized properly. Off we go to the accessory store based upon another salesperson's recommendation and promotion.

No one has recommended food. I am getting hungry. So I stop the mall security guard and ask, "Where can I get some quick calories? I am weak. I have been fasting for almost two hours."

The security recommends the "Donut Warehouse Outlet." And off I go to get some real food.

Did you notice?

Every person that we talked to at the shopping mall recommended and promoted something ... and didn't get paid for it.

Yes, most people do network marketing every day, but they fail to get paid for their recommending and promoting efforts.

Here are a few more examples:

- Recommending a playground for the children.

- Recommending a hotel with a great view.

- Recommending an upcoming concert.

- Recommending a fun activity for the weekend.

- Recommending a brand of clothes.

- Recommending your beautician.

- Recommending an airline.

- Recommending a lawyer.

- Recommending a dentist.

- Recommending your favorite evening television show.

- Recommending a fat-free dessert.

- Recommending a great view.

- Recommending a music teacher.

- Recommending some exciting night clubs.

- Recommending a computer chair.

- Recommending a good babysitter.

- Recommending where to find the best burgers.

- Recommending a good lawn maintenance service.

- Recommending a good place to play golf.

- Recommending a cruise.

This is what network marketing looks like in real life. Everyone is recommending things. It is part of our nature to share information about resources that can help other people.

We recommend, the prospect listens ... and then it is up to the prospect to decide if our recommendation will serve him or not. This is a recommendation, not an order!

Our prospects will make decisions based upon what is happening in their lives, so don't feel offended if prospects don't like the dessert you recommended because they are allergic to milk. Or, don't take it personally if a prospect hates dancing and refuses to go to your favorite nightclub.

So, how do I get paid for this?

Once your prospects understand this concept, they will ask you the following question:

"If I am doing the work **anyway**, how do I collect?"

This means you have completed the first phase of educating your prospects and new distributors. Now your prospects and distributors no longer reject the idea of network marketing as being strange or unusual. They **respect** network marketing and they want to know how they can collect for their efforts.

But it gets even better!

Have you ever had a distributor quit? (I know, of course you haven't, but you might have read about it.)

Anyway, if you teach this principle, you insulate your distributor from the negative influences of worthless brothers-in-law.

Let's say that your new distributor comes home from an opportunity meeting and announces to his family and worthless brother-in-law:

"I just joined network marketing. I am going to be rich! This is the happiest day of my life!"

What does his worthless brother-in-law want to do? He wants to depress your new distributor and tell him how stupid he is. So the worthless brother-in-law says:

"Boy, are you stupid. Look at you. You are going to be doing network marketing every day ... and getting paid for it. But not me! Oh no! I am going to do network marketing every day and not get paid for it! So what do you think about that, eh?"

Well, what will your new distributor think? He will be thinking:

"Wow! My worthless brother-in-law is such an idiot. I guess I could invest a few minutes and explain to him that he is doing network marketing and not getting paid for it, and potentially change his financial life forever. Or ... maybe I won't tell him anything and let him suffer in misery and poverty for the rest of his life."

Do you see how we have protected our new distributor from the negative influences of others? He has this protection because he understands this awesome first sentence.

It gets better and better!

There are even more benefits of understanding the first sentence, "Most people do network marketing every day, but they just don't get paid for it."

For instance, your new distributor no longer has to look for prospects, rent leads, or run ads. Why?

Because almost everyone is already doing network marketing every day, but they just aren't getting paid for it.

This means that everyone your new distributor comes into contact with is already fully qualified to collect, fully qualified to do this business – because they are **already** doing it!

Your new distributor only has to notify the prospect that he can collect a check for what he is already doing, or continue doing network marketing for free.

This makes it easy to contact everyone. You no longer have to convince people to join network marketing, because they have **already** joined.

You are simply letting them know they can pick up a check.

The fear of rejection simply **melts away** when we understand this principle. And even if the prospect insists on not collecting a check, we don't feel bad. We gave the prospect a choice.

We are not **responsible** for the decisions our prospects make in their lives. We are only obligated to give them the choices. After all, we aren't responsible for the spouse they chose or the house they chose, right?

So here is a test you can use to determine if your new distributor understands this first sentence.

Suppose your new distributor says:

"I just don't have anybody to talk to. Where can I find some hot prospects?"

Well, if your new distributor says that, he **doesn't** understand this opening first sentence.

Commit to teaching this first sentence to your new distributors until they "get it."

Say your first sentence ... and listen.

The new distributor asked, "How do you know what to say to people? How do you know which benefit to talk about?"

For new distributors this seems hard. For experienced networkers, we automatically know what to talk about. Here is how we do it.

People will only want to join our business if it solves a **problem**. So how do we know what problems prospects have? Easy.

We listen. People love to talk about their problems. Many times, the first things they tell strangers are all about the problems in their lives.

So all we have to do is keep quiet and listen. That is hard for some distributors who are eager to start talking **AT** prospects about their business.

The purpose of business is to solve problems for prospects. So we shouldn't even begin to talk about our business until we know which problems our business can solve for our prospects.

We talk too much, and listen too little.

Everyone knows that.

Great first sentences are a great reason to delay your sales presentations.

With the first glimmer of an opening, amateur network marketers jump into their full presentation. If the prospect takes a breath, well, that looks like the time to pull out the flip chart or PowerPoint and start a quick 40-minute monologue of the benefits of the business opportunity.

I have been on the receiving end of plenty of these presentations. I bet you have, too. And it's not very pleasant.

Most of these presentations end in failure.

Why?

Because the prospect doesn't feel a sincere or **desperate** need for this "wonderful" opportunity.

Professionals know that it is useless to provide a solution when the prospect doesn't perceive a problem.

In other words, **before we begin** our presentation, we must first convince the prospect that he wants to fix a problem.

That's called ...

Digging deeper for more pain.

And the deeper you dig **before** you begin your presentation, the easier the presentation becomes. Offering to solve the prospect's problems too soon will work against you because the prospect will only see you as a boring intrusion in his life.

**An easy way to dig for problems is
with a great first sentence.**

Let's say that your prospect has a problem with not having enough time. He commutes long hours to and from work, and has to work most Saturdays to keep up with the increasing workload. Yes, our prospect has a time problem. Here are four types of first sentences that could help.

**#1. Ask questions to identify a problem
or deficiency in the prospect's life.**

* "If you had Saturdays off, what would you do?"

* "How long has it been since you attended one of your son's baseball games?"

* "Do you remember what it was like when you and your wife had time to go out to dinner and a movie?"

* "Is your vacation time a quality experience with the family, or just catching up on everything you have put off during the year?"

What a great way to start a conversation. Just one simple sentence, and prospects convince themselves that they are looking for a solution.

**#2. Go deeper to point out the
serious nature of the problem.**

* "What does your son say when you tell him you can't go to his baseball game?"

* "Do you feel stressed because you have no time for yourself? No time for hobbies? Not enough time with your spouse and family?"

* "Do you ever feel that life is passing you by and that you'll never travel and see those places you dreamed about when you were in school?"

#3. Review the serious consequences
of not solving the problem.

* "Because your son is too young to understand why you can't come to his baseball games, what effect will this have on him?"

* "How do you feel every day at work knowing that your schedule may never change?"

* "Do you feel like you might be waiting too long to enjoy life? That you might be too old when you finally get some free time?"

#4. Check to see if there will be additional problems
caused by not solving the present problem.

* "If you don't start spending some quality time with your family, what do you think is going to happen?"

* "How long will your spouse be happy with your present schedule?"

* "Do you think your body will hold up to this constant stress?"

And now it's a better time to start our presentation.

Our first sentence has helped the prospect identify a problem and feel a need to solve the problem. Now the prospect will be attentive to our proposed solutions.

See the difference? It's easier when the prospect wants to hear what we have to say.

First: Great first sentence.

Second: Listen.

Third: Then present.

Easy.

Impress your prospects with fortune cookies.

Your opportunity meeting is over. Your guest is munching on a few snacks in the back of the room. Your guest picks up a fortune cookie, breaks it open to read the message, and the message says:

"A wonderful opportunity is coming your way, so don't miss your chance of a lifetime."

Your prospect turns to you, smiles, and says:

"So how can I get started tonight?"

Wow! If only your prospect was **lucky** enough to get a fortune cookie with that message. But you don't have to rely on luck. You can create your own custom, individually-wrapped fortune cookies with **your** unique message. Fortune cookies with personalized messages are a bargain!

I just searched "personalize fortune cookies" on the Internet and got these prices:

12 cookies $15

50 cookies $20

100 cookies $25

250 cookies $45

500 cookies $59

1000 cookies $119

2500 cookies $230

5000 cookies $450 (That is only nine cents a cookie! Some business cards are more expensive than that!)

How could you use these fortune cookies?

Let's make a list:

* Pass them out at trade shows.

* Leave them with your business card at networking events (your contacts will remember you.)

* Leave one with a prospect after your presentation.

* Pass them out in the lunchroom at work.

* Bring them to family reunions.

* Distribute them at parties.

What can you say in your custom fortune cookies?

Here are some examples:

* "A failure is someone who doesn't try."

* "A wise man takes opportunities when available."

* "Most people do network marketing every day. Why not get paid for what you're doing?"

* "A happy family owns its own business and its life."

* "There is a new car in your future."

* "You will be very rich and happy – if you have the courage to act."

* "You will meet many new friends in your new ventures."

* "Opportunities are only available to those who act now!"

* "This cookie will make you fat. I have the antidote!"

* "40% off your first order!"

* "You are paying too much for your mobile phone."

* "A job guarantees you will be broke. Do more."

* "Avoid Chinese food. Try our gourmet food."

* "Do not mistake a job for an opportunity."

* "If you work hard, then your boss will have a big house for his retirement."

* "If you are unhappy on Monday mornings, change careers."

I am sure you can think of many more great messages for your custom fortune cookies.

Sorting prospects with first sentences.

I am often asked:

"If I am sorting through prospects, I need to know if the prospect is **qualified** to do my business and **wants** to do my business. What should I look for?"

The answer is simple. And if you have read my book, Sponsoring Magic, you know the simple sorting technique.

#1. The prospect must have desire.

If the prospect doesn't want to try, you are wasting your time. So try a first sentence that asks a question such as:

"Do you want to earn some extra money?"

"Would it be okay if you got an extra paycheck?"

"Would you like to fire your boss?"

The question isn't important. The **answer** is what is important. So listen closely. If the prospect says:

"Well, I was looking for something I could do from home, while watching television, that wasn't hard, and I certainly don't want to talk to people or be a salesman, and if I could get paid in advance ..."

You have your answer. Move on. No matter how easy you make it for this prospect, there isn't much of a future here.

But, what if the prospect answers this way?

"More money? Yes! I have bills to pay, and I am not going to get a raise this year. I want to do something to get out of this rut. Tell me more."

Now this is easy. This prospect passes the desire test, and you can invest some time with this prospect.

When we first start, we tend to take anyone who will talk to us. That is not so bad in the beginning; we do need practice. But eventually these types of lazy prospects will take up all of our time. They drag us down with their negativity. This means we won't have the quality time to find new and better prospects.

So the first rule in sorting for prospects is to check for **desire**.

The second rule is equally simple.

Check for time.

Simply ask a time-related question such as:

"Can you set aside five to ten hours a week?"

Again the question isn't important, it is the **answer**.

If the prospect answers:

"Well, on Monday night I watch football, Tuesday night is family night where the family goes out and I can watch television in peace, Wednesday night is my bowling league, and then there is the weekend ... I guess I could set aside an hour or two on Thursday nights every so often."

Hint: You might want to look for a better prospect to work with.

Now, of course some people can do more in one hour than others can do in a week, so what we really are checking for here is if they will truly **set aside** some time for the business.

Everyone has 24 hours in a day. It is how they choose to spend their time that is important. So listen to see if they have the desire to spend it building a business.

Two qualifications (desire + time) = great prospect.

These are the two essentials for having a great prospect. They have a strong desire to earn some extra money, and they are willing to invest some time into building their business. Without these two important ingredients, we are probably wasting our time. So make sure to check for these qualifications first.

Turning your first sentence into a simple "sorting" question will make this process easy.

How to turn down prospects gracefully.

Make our first sentence negative?

Yes.

It is yet another strategy that we can use to make our first sentence do almost all the work.

In the beginning of our network marketing career, we will sponsor anything that moves. If they breathe, they qualify.

Why? Because we have to start somewhere. We have to begin working with **someone**. We can't build a business without people.

Later, as our network marketing career progresses, we can be a bit more selective about who we sponsor into our business.

Why? Because if we are smart, we only want friends in our organization. We don't want:

* Recreational complainers.

* Professional victims.

* Negative whiners.

* Lonely people who will only dump their troubles on us daily.

Here is one way to be a bit more selective.

On a flight to Singapore, I sat next to a lady who was a non-stop talker. Not only did she talk about petty things such as what the soap opera characters might do next week, but she argued with the passenger next to her whenever he had an opinion. So, I thought to myself, "If I pretend to sleep, maybe she won't notice me."

Well, that didn't bother her. She started talking to me about how the world didn't agree with her, how the airline was bad, how the food was bad, how her fellow passengers were jerks (I guess that included me), and how the world was such a lousy place to live in.

Hmmm, let's see here. If I sponsored her, I would have to listen to her for the rest of my life. I immediately pre-judged her as someone who shouldn't be in my network marketing business.

Finally, after a 30-minute monologue on the depressing state of current events, she asked me what I did for a living. Aaaacckkk!

Thinking fast, I replied with one of my favorite phrases: "It's top secret. If I told you, I would have to kill you."

Unfortunately, that wasn't good enough. She replied, "Well, couldn't you just give me a little hint and only wound me?"

The point of this story is that you don't want everyone in your business. And, if you are somewhat selective, then people will **come to you** and ask if they can qualify. By taking the opportunity **away** from people, sometimes they actually **want it more**.

I can't explain this phenomenon of human nature. I can only report it. That is why you see ad headlines that say:

* For Winners Only!

* Only Three Openings Available!

* Experienced Professionals Only!

* Leaders Wanted -- Followers Need Not Apply!

What do these ad headlines have in common? They usually draw many more quality responses than headlines that tell the reader, "If you breathe, please come and apply. We are desperate for anybody."

So, how selective or exclusive should your offer be? That is up to you. But, don't limit this technique to your headlines only.

Starting a presentation with a qualifying first sentence.

Try this. Make your first sentence this question:

"Are you committed enough to invest $1,500 monthly for six months to start and establish your own business?"

I like this question. It not only gets a commitment from the prospect for a **money** and **time** investment, it also gives the prospect a realistic vision for six months.

The $1,500 monthly investment sounds steep, but if a prospect really wanted to open any business, the requirements would actually be much higher. Of course, if the money commitment was too large for the prospect, you could reduce the monetary requirements by asking for more sweat equity and effort on his part.

By the time you ask for $50 for a distributor kit at the end of your presentation, the $50 appears to be pocket change compared to the $1,500 original commitment.

Opportunity meetings.

For instance, you could start your opportunity meetings with this first sentence:

"If you are afraid to be your own boss, and are addicted to a job taking orders from a boss, then relax and spend the next 30 minutes messaging your friends on your phone."

The listener now has a choice. "Do I disqualify myself, give up on my dreams, and just wait to die? Or, do I put my phone aside and look for ways to change my life?"

How about the close at the end of the meeting?

You could start your close at the end of your opportunity meeting presentation with a great sentence. You could use an "exclusive close" by saying:

"If you are a procrastinator, or unable to act on profitable ideas ... or are unwilling to change your future, then this opportunity is not for you. This opportunity is the fast track to success for coachable, motivated people who want a better future."

This type of "exclusive close" gets fence-sitters, the undecided prospects, to act now. They want to move up and be part of a group of winners ... and here is their chance.

Try some first sentences and headlines that motivate prospects to come to you.

Positive opening questions.

Prospects need to see the benefits of your offer in their minds. Sure, you can put those benefits in their minds. But instead, why not make the vision more powerful by having them put their own versions in their minds?

You can do this with just one powerful first sentence.

We can get our prospects to mentally sell themselves and see the benefits of our offer with this simple question:

"What would happen if ...?"

Here are some examples:

* "What would happen if you didn't have to wake up every morning to go to work?"

* "What would happen if you had more holiday time with the family?"

* "What would happen if you didn't have to spend hours commuting every week?"

* "What would happen if you had an extra paycheck every month?"

* "What would happen if you could retire next year?"

* "What would happen if you had a bigger paycheck for your family?"

51

* "What would happen if you could take a five-star vacation with the kids?"

* "What would happen if you had more time to work on your dreams?"

* "What would happen if you could lose 12 pounds this month?"

* "What would happen if you could help your daughter get rid of her acne?"

* "What would happen if you got a huge discount on your electric bill?"

* "What would happen if you could sell your alarm clock to your neighbor?"

* "What would happen if you could keep wrinkles away an extra 15 years?"

* "What would happen if you didn't have to make car payments ever again?"

* "What would happen if you could work from your home and didn't have to send your baby to daycare?"

Just start with this simple question as your first sentence, then relax. Let the prospects think and talk ... and sell themselves before you begin your second sentence.

Negative opening questions.

Prospects also need to visualize the penalty for staying in their present circumstances. Many prospects continue to live in high levels of dissatisfaction and pain because they are afraid to take action. They prefer not to think about the penalty. Instead, they resist change and hope they don't have to look at something new.

They are afraid to open up their minds to change!

We may have to use a powerful first sentence to shock their minds into assessing their current misery. We can help them assess their dissatisfaction by using this one simple question:

"Are you okay with ...?"

Here are some examples:

* "Are you okay with 40 years of hard labor to help your boss get rich?"

* "Are you okay with five days of every week being taken from you?"

* "Are you okay with waking up early to work hard for someone else?"

* "Are you okay with taking orders from someone else for 40 years?"

* "Are you okay with someone else telling you how much money you can earn?"

* "Are you okay with only a few weeks of vacation time every year?"

* "Are you okay with giving up your freedom to do the work you hate?"

* "Are you okay with working in a job that you have no passion for?"

* "Are you okay with giving up your dreams to work on your supervisor's dreams?"

* "Are you okay with begging someone else for a raise?"

* "Are you okay with only limited time to travel?"

* "Are you okay with your skin wrinkling a little bit more every night?"

* "Are you okay with a low metabolism so everything seems to stick to your hips?"

* "Are you okay with paying huge mobile telephone bills?"

* "Are you okay with never having enough money to afford a home?"

Just start with this **negative** question as your first sentence, then relax. Let the prospects think and talk ... and sell themselves before you say your second sentence.

Need another formula?

Use "Get rid of _____" to soothe your prospects' pain.

Here are some examples:

* "Get rid of your boss forever."

* "Get rid of your alarm clock forever."

* "Get rid of old, wrinkly skin with this special serum."

* "Get rid of car payments now."

* "Get rid of unwanted fat with this herbal formula."

* "Get rid of those extra charges on your utility bill."

* "Eat this breakfast and get rid of hunger pains and cravings."

* "Want to get rid of those wasteful commuting hours?"

* "Want to get rid of sleepless nights?"

Just one more formula. :)

* "Can you spot these seven signs of a dead-end job?"

* "Can you spot these four signs of an impending heart attack?"

* "Can you see these four signs of prematurely-aging skin?"

* "Can you taste these four unhealthy chemicals in your food?"

* "Can you feel these three early signs of burnout?"

Enough negativity. Let's move on.

To get referrals ...

Many times you can get more prospects for your opportunity by talking about your product or service. By simply asking for referrals, prospects might say that they are personally interested, or send you to a prospect who is highly interested.

Examples of referral questions
to start your conversation.

If you sold electricity, you could say:

"Do you know anyone who wants a discount on their electric bill?"

The prospect can easily mention a few referrals for you. This is rejection-free, non-confrontational, and fun. And the best part is ... your prospect might become a distributor once he realizes all the potential customers that he knows.

This is one of the easiest ways to get lots of leads for your business. Here are some examples of questions you can use for other products and services:

* "Do you know anyone who wants to lose weight without heavy exercising?"

* "Do you know anyone who loves to exercise and eat healthy?"

* "Do you know anyone who feels tired in the morning?"

* "Do you know anyone frustrated with skin problems?"

* "Do you know anyone who would like to travel for less?"

* "Do you know anyone who likes taking good care of their skin?"

* "Do you know anyone who loves to travel?"

* "Do you know anyone who loves to drink coffee?"

And yes, you can use this type of opening question for your opportunity also.

* "Do you know anyone who hates being awakened by an alarm clock?"

* "Do you know anyone who needs to earn a lot more money?"

* "Do you know anyone who likes to save on their taxes?"

* "Do you know anyone who loves helping other people?"

* "Do you know anyone who hates rush hour commuting?"

* "Do you know anyone who works six or seven days a week?"

Remember, each prospect you talk to knows at least 200 people that you don't. When you ask these types of questions, your prospect can point you to the best possible candidates.

Are headlines first sentences?

Of course.

You want your prospect to be **leaning forward** with interest, not **leaning backwards** with resistance.

I can't overemphasize the value of a great first sentence. Your prospect makes the decision to be interested in **seconds**. Your window into your prospect's mind is very, very small.

Think about it. You make the same quick decisions, too. If a telephone solicitor calls you, haven't you already made up your mind in the first few seconds?

Instead of wasting time on perfecting slide #43 in your PowerPoint presentation, consider this. If you put the same effort into improving your first sentence or headline, would the payoff be bigger?

Have you ever read a newspaper?

How do you read the newspaper? Do you start at the upper left-hand corner and read everything until you get to the bottom right-hand corner of the last page?

I don't think so. I bet you only read certain articles.

And how do you choose which articles to read?

By the headlines.

If the headline grabs your interest, you read the article. If the headline has no interest to you, you **skip** the article. You simply **scan** the newspaper headlines and make split-second decisions on what you'll read.

Same with books.

As you walk through the aisles of bookstores, how do you choose which book to browse?

By the title (headline).

Many great books were never read because they had a bad title. First impressions count!

Your prospects scan what you say.

That's right. If your first sentence is boring, then just like the newspaper, the prospect will turn his attention elsewhere. We tune out boring messages. We think of other things while that pushy salesman is talking.

Your prospects scan your prospecting materials.

Your prospects **scan** your headlines and first sentences and decide if they will read your fancy material ... or turn their attention to other events in their lives. This means you must put your best benefits, your best-selling copy, and your best efforts into your headlines.

Forget our stupid opinions.

We are different. We are entrepreneurs, network marketers, and we believe in opportunity and positive thinking. We think ... differently!

Our prospects may be job holders, crushed by society, overworked, underpaid, skeptical, self-sabotaging and might even have a terrible, negative outlook on life.

Our prospects think ... totally differently!

So who is more qualified to pick the better first sentence or headline?

Prospects, of course. We can't let our egos decide which first sentence or headline to use. We are not trying to attract or convince people like us. We have **already** joined.

Twenty years ago I conducted this experiment, just to see which headlines would be most attractive to prospects. People were shocked when I published the results. The lessons from this experiment are huge, and effective, if we use them.

Here is the experiment I did to see which headline I should use for a promotional campaign that I was planning. This experiment was done before the Internet was readily accessible, but now with the Internet, this experiment would be even easier!

How to choose the best first sentence or headline.

Imagine I approached you and said:

"I am conducting a survey, could you spare just a minute? I will send you a free business report as a thank-you for your help."

You might politely say:

"One minute? Well, okay. What is the survey?"

I would present my survey and say:

"I am testing the popularity of six of our business reports. Here are the six reports we offer:

1. How to build a part-time business while keeping your present job.

2. The insecurity of corporate America and what you can do about it.

3. How to get rich using sweat equity instead of risking large amounts of cash.

4. The truth about owning a business: The problems and the benefits.

5. Single-income job strategy. Why it fails. What can be done.

6. Leveraging your efforts. A unique method for residual income.

"Please check the report you think would be most popular, and list your occupation. I will mail you the report you chose as a thank-you for your time. Please write your name and mailing address here at the bottom of this form."

Choose now.

Okay, make your choice from the six titles above.

Report #1? Report #4? Which report would you choose?

Please remember which report you wanted the most as we continue.

There were several reasons for this project. Let's start with the first purpose of this exercise.

Even if you can't prospect, can't recruit, and can't sponsor, at least you can take a survey.

Yes, you could make up copies of this little survey, put them on a clipboard, and take surveys from the general public. What would happen?

* You would get lots of pre-qualified prospects and some distributors.

* You have just captured the name and address or email address of the prospects.

* You know which report they chose and thus their motivation.

* And it shouldn't be hard to follow up with a phone call, a letter, or an email.

When you mailed or emailed the four-page report of their choice, you could include an audio or some literature about your opportunity. Certainly if prospects want to know how to get residual income, they won't be offended with extra information with their report.

If you are more aggressive, you can telephone your prospect a few days after mailing the report. Most people have listed telephone numbers and you already have their name and address. In my survey I didn't ask for telephone numbers as I was looking to get the maximum number of surveys. Of course you could add a place for the prospect's telephone number if you wanted.

If 50 prospects fill out this form and choose a report that interests them, don't you think you would at least sponsor four or five of these pre-qualified opportunity-seekers?

But where do I get those six reports?

No problem. You can have just one report ... and six different title pages. You see, all the headlines (report titles) really **say the same thing**. Simply put a different title page on top of your report and mail it to the prospect with your company information.

You only need **one** report to make this survey-prospecting method work. And, you can customize the report for your business or business philosophy.

If you don't have a report written yet, do it now. Surely there is someone in your upline or downline with some writing skills. If not, contact a professional writer by searching the Internet. Many times you can get this report for as little as five dollars.

The point is: You only need one report and you are on your way.

But that is not the real reason for the experiment!

This experiment is all about ... **"Testing."**

If you don't test what you are doing, you are making a big mistake. And I know we have all heard that many times before ... and I know we still don't do it ... because normally it is hard, time-consuming, and boring to test things. And, how do you test something anyway?

Lots of network marketing distributors call me for advice on advertising techniques. I recently received a call from a distributor who complained, "My advertisement is not pulling as well as I had hoped. Why don't more readers respond?"

Good question. A very good question. My reply?

I asked the caller these questions:

* How did you come up with your headline?

* Did you test the headline elsewhere and measure the results?

* Did you run your headline by a few friends to get their opinion?

* What other headlines did you test before you chose this headline?

* What did your testing show before you invested in your present ad campaign?

* Did you hire a professional copywriter to help you create this headline?

* Did you study some books to learn the basics of headline composition?

So, how did he choose his headline?

His answer: "Oh, I just thought it up."

Wrong answer.

Amateur research and preparation will bring amateur results. If you wanted to recruit successfully, you would invest in some books or courses about recruiting techniques. If you wanted to retail successfully, you would invest in a sales course.

So it follows that if you want to advertise and promote successfully, you should at least invest in some books to learn the basics. The "Oh, I just thought it up" method won't get you the results you want.

And if you read some books and take some courses, the number one thing that you will learn is ...

Testing! That's the key.

So how do you test a headline? Do you mail two different headlines to 5,000 people and measure the results? That works. Unfortunately, that will cost you thousands of dollars in postage. And if you did it by email, you would have to rent a couple hundred thousand names to get the same amount of responses. Why? Because much of our email goes to spam folders.

Is there a way we can test less expensively? Yes!

Now here's the good part ...

Imagine we wanted to test six different headlines. We know which headline we like the most, but we aren't the prospects. We think differently. We respond to different things.

A good example is fishing. If we wanted to catch a fish, we wouldn't put a candy bar on the hook. We would put a slimy, ugly, terrible-tasting worm on the hook because that is what the fish wants. Remember, when we fish, it is not what we want that matters, it is what the fish wants that matters.

Now, how are we going to test six different headlines with "live" prospects? Hmmm. Could we put together a survey and use the six headlines as report titles? Then, could we get "live" prospects to pick which headline (report title) that they like best?

Wow!!!! Now we are on to something!

Live data! True testing! And it is cheap!

We need to have inexpensive and **effectively-tested** headlines for our advertisements, for our opening statements in an opportunity meeting, for face-to-face prospecting conversations, etc.

And now for the results. Open the envelope, please!

Ready for the results from the six headlines (report titles)?

First, which one did you choose? And, does it really matter which one you choose, or is it the prospect's preference that counts?

"Riches to Rags" if you picked the wrong headline!

I used this survey extensively for six weeks.

Where did I test these six headlines?

At recruiting workshops, at marketing workshops, at opportunity meetings, and even at the shopping mall.

I thought that the results would be quite different at each location. Surely, a power network marketer at a workshop would look at these titles quite differently from a mall shopper. Was I surprised at the results?

You bet. I was stunned! I found out that prospects don't think like me. (That is probably good!)

So, here are the startling results for the six headlines. I have condensed the data for easy comparison, so here is the result per 100 people surveyed.

Report #1: 37 requests

Report #2: Only 2 requests

Report #3: 10 requests

Report #4: 9 requests

Report #5: 3 requests

Report #6: 39 requests

Do you see the two big winners?

Report #1: "How to build a part-time business while keeping your present job."

Report #6: "Leveraging your efforts. A unique method for residual income."

These headlines really drew the interest of the prospects. (Remember, this experiment was done in 1995. Today, the words used and interest levels might be different. For example, you could say, "Life hacks for a part-time business." That would be trendy today, but maybe not next year.)

Back to the two big winners ...

Important data? You bet!

Suppose you chose Report #5:

"Single income job strategy. Why it fails. What can be done." as your headline.

Your response would be almost nothing.

You would say: "Advertising doesn't work!"

Well, advertising does work. You just picked a bad headline. If you would have picked Report #6 as your headline (39 requests vs. the 3 requests for Report #5), **you would have received 13 times the response, 13 times the new distributor enrollments, and 13 times the bonus check!!!**

Now we are talking important results. For instance, let's say your present network marketing bonus check is $1,000 and you are working hard. Did it ever occur to you that maybe you could be saying the wrong thing in your presentation? Did you test your presentation?

Maybe what you're saying is like Report #5. Could you change to a different presentation that would give you 13 times the results? Instead of earning $1,000 ... **you could be earning $13,000 with the same effort - if you tested.**

I think testing is important.

I know you are not testing now. We are all so busy building a business that we forget to test, test, and test some more. I know you could double or triple your bonus check easily if you tested. I have given you one easy way to test.

The rest is up to you.

There is a lot more that we can learn from this experiment ... but the big lesson is that you can earn up to 13 times more money just by testing.

Let's quickly look at some other lessons from this six-headline (report title) survey.

Mini-lesson #1: I personally wrote all six headlines. I thought they were all great. I was **wrong** four out of six times. Now, I think I am a pretty good copywriter and judge of human nature. It is humbling, but I am wrong 66% of the time. Ouch! The reason I have experienced some success in marketing is that I know I am wrong most of the time and I test to find the right answer. Then I use the right answer. That is why I am always field-testing before I write anything. You see, there is theory ... and then there is the truth.

Mini-lesson #2: I tested this survey with many different groups. I thought the mall shopper would want a different report than the experienced networker. Again, I was **wrong**. In this case, almost everyone wanted Report #1 or Report #6. Usually there would be a difference. In this case, there was no difference. You have to test.

Mini-lesson #3: If I wanted a killer headline, or if I wanted a great message to invite someone to an opportunity meeting, what would I say? I would combine Report #1 and Report #6 into a headline and a sub-headline. I would say:

**How to build a part-time business
while keeping your present job!**

**Leverage your efforts with a
unique method for residual income.**

It is a longer headline than most, but I am sure it would work better than my other four headlines - because it is **tested**.

Mini-lesson #4: The survey asked for the prospect's occupation. Why? Your testing might show that real estate investors prefer Report #3: How to get rich using sweat equity instead of risking large amounts of cash. That's important if you later decided to advertise in a real estate publication or website. You would already know what attracts the readers of that publication or website.

By keeping track of the different occupations, you might pick up some interesting trends. A word of caution: Don't over-analyze or micro-analyze your results. Just evaluate the obvious trends.

Mini-lesson #5: Many distributors create their own websites or marketing audios. Have you noticed something?

Many of these presentations start with an overview of the loss of conventional jobs, the changing paradigm, etc. Now, look at Report #2: "The insecurity of corporate America and what you can do about it." How many prospects chose that report? Only 2 out of 100! Does that tell us something?

Maybe our prospects don't want to hear that message. Maybe they already know that. Maybe that message is just boring and they want to know what else we can do for them "right now."

Judging from the results of our survey, I think I might change some of those lifestyle recruiting audios I've heard and make the headline: "Greed, leverage, obscene residual incomes." Hey, I am just adjusting to the wishes of the prospects we surveyed. :)

A final word: T-E-S-T!!

If you can't take the time to test six different approaches or headlines, then you deserve to be making only 10% of what you **could** be collecting in monthly bonus checks.

I even had a friend, Chuck Huckaby, test the experiment. Yes, he tested the test! He wrote me:

"When I changed the numbers on the survey responses, the same headlines won again ... even at different positions according to my online survey."

So, what about you? Are you testing? Are you taking advantage of the leverage we discussed?

If not, survey, survey, and survey. Remember, the worst that can happen is that you get a lot of new distributors with your test. The best that can happen is that you isolate the winning benefit or phrase that doubles or even triples your income in 30 days.

Some "tested" first sentences that work.

Could your prospecting and retailing first sentences use some improvement?

Here is just one case study that again shows the difference a sentence can make.

Years ago, *Movieline Magazine* increased their new business gross response by 7.5% and net response by 29.6% by changing the first sentence on its direct mail envelope from:

"Do you have the guts ..."

to

"Toss this envelope ... if you're looking for a safe, sweet movie magazine that flatters the pants off Hollywood ..."

Think about it. Just this one simple change made a 29.6% difference.

Wouldn't you like your bonus check to **increase** 29.6% by only changing a few words?

How much more effective would your sponsoring be if you had a "killer" first sentence that stopped prospects in their tracks? And what if you passed your new first sentence on to your downline? Could you get excited about how much faster your business would grow?

So why not take a little time today to improve your first sentence?

Do you need a little inspiration?

Here are some first sentences and headlines to get you thinking:

* "Pure water for only four cents a gallon!" (If someone is buying bottled water, this is almost a sure sale.)

* "Stop smoking -- or die!" (Pretty drastic, but does get their attention.)

* "How to make money every time your neighbor uses the telephone." (Curiosity sells. We want to know.)

* "This is the herb that weight-loss doctors give their wives to reduce fat." (See, we knew there was a secret being withheld from us fat people. It isn't our fault. We just didn't know about this herb ...)

* "How to feel like you are 16 years old again ... but with better judgment." (In this case, a bit of humor works. The prospect relives some of his memories and feels good. Watch for a smile.)

* "Eat cookies – lose weight!" (The word "cookie" removes all logic from the fat prospect's mind. Yes, we want to try this diet!)

* "If home is where your heart is, shouldn't your business be there, too?" (A bit cerebral. Forces the prospect to ponder this statement. Probably not good for a first sentence, but it could be a strong headline that demands the prospect's attention.

* "There I was at 15,000 feet, both engines on fire and my parachute in the laundry ..." (I had to read on. Great attention-grabber. Can you imagine starting your speech or meeting with this sentence? Everyone would be sitting on the edge of their seats.)

Can you come up with your own
first sentences and headlines?

It just takes a little imagination and practice. But once you get that great first sentence, and pass it on to your downline, watch out! Sales volume and recruiting can surge.

We spend entirely too much time on perfecting the rest of our presentation – but the truth is, if our first sentence isn't good, no one is listening to the rest of our presentation.

And you don't have to limit your first sentence to face-to-face presentations. You can use a great first sentence or headline on telephone calls, email subject lines, first sentences of your sales letters, business cards, brochures, posters, ads, etc.

So it makes sense to invest a lot of time to get a good clear message into your first sentence.

Want some more tested examples to get you thinking? Here are a few more of my favorite first sentences and headlines.

* "Fire your boss!"

* "Start your own business - with no overhead!"

* "Get a $400-a-month raise without telling your boss!"

* "The two foods you should eat every morning."

* "Three reasons you should fire your boss now."

* "How two mailroom employees from Winchester show ordinary people how to retire in just 3 1/2 years."

* "How to lose 15 pounds of fat in 30 days - without exercise!"

* "Here are 10 out of 29 reasons you should join us now!"

* "Do you know the three secrets networking pros use to kickstart their business?"

* "How a legal secretary from Norway shows people how to get an extra check in their mailbox every week."

* "If your job pays less than $50,000 a year, you qualify to receive this free special report."

* "You are only one good opportunity away from a million-dollar fortune."

* "Five new reasons you'll want to be at Thursday night's business briefing."

* "Do you know the best way to start a home-based business for less than $250?"

* "Three miracle exercises that reduce cellulite."

* "86-year-old granny starts second career as a part-time breakdancing instructor."

* "Secret food helps burn body fat while you drive to work."

We could go on and on, but you should be inspired by now to start creating your own first sentences. So grab a pencil or pen, and begin writing down those great first sentence ideas for your business and products.

Who knows?

You might come up with a million-dollar winner! Your downline would appreciate that.

Guessing ... stinks.

"I thought up the headline myself. I guess at least I would answer this ad."

A distributor picks the first sentence or headline by saying to himself: "That sounds good."

No testing. No research. Just a warm fuzzy sensation that makes the distributor feel good.

Do you choose a first sentence or headline because it sounds good to you?

* My growling stomach sounds good to me because I love to have an excuse to eat. However, my growling stomach may not sound good to **you**.

* Rap or heavy metal music may sound good to you ... but does it sound good to your prospects?

* Tuna casserole, beer, and baked beans may sound good to you ... but will it sound good to everyone else?

You see, the prospects are buying the first sentence or headline, not you. So your job is to provide what the prospect wants, not what you like.

Why test? Because one headline may pull twice the response of another headline. That will save you a lot of money and time. Or, if it is a good first sentence, you will get twice as many prospects, and they will have open minds instead of closed minds.

I get to talk with many network marketers. Out of ten network marketers, guess how many tell me they have tested what they say?

The answer? **Zero!**

These amateurs are your competition!

You can rest securely at night knowing that your competition is **just thinking up stuff**, hoping that they might get lucky. That is why network marketing can be so easy ... there is so little competition!

Your competition isn't willing to do the work to become successful. Are you willing to test what you say or do you want to become part of the "average" competition?

It's your money. Spend it as you like.

Take this test ... and wager your money!

Here are five sets of competing headlines. Your mission is to pick which headlines got the best response. Ready?

* * *

Set #1.

A. How to get the other 240,000,000 Americans to join your MLM program.

B. Amazing 24-page book brings hot prospects to you.

Set #2.

A. Special $99 "Fast Start Training Package" saves you $34.75.

B. The complete business-in-a-box for only $99.

Set #3.

A. The art of controversy.

B. How to argue logically.

Set #4.

A. Never diet again.

B. Amazing cookie manages your weight.

Set #5.

A. Financial freedom through network marketing.

B. Are you tired of working for someone else?

* * *

Okay, have you chosen the best headline in each set? Good.

Now, take some money out of your wallet or purse. Let's say about $1,000 in cash. We are going to make an imaginary wager.

Would you bet your $1,000 in cash that you got the answers right in each of the five sets of headlines?

Probably not.

You are not 100% sure which headlines pulled the best so you will want to play it safe and not risk your $1,000 in cash. I don't blame you. Losing $1,000 on a wager can be scary.

Would you wager your car? Your home? Your business? Probably not.

Hah!

However, that is what you are doing every time you advertise or promote. You are making a wager with your money that you can somehow be lucky and pick a winning headline or first sentence.

Sometimes you are lucky; most times you are not.

What happens when you aren't lucky? You lose $100, or $1,000, or even more because you didn't take the time to test your headline. Or worse yet, you lose a prospect that could have earned you thousands every month, because you didn't have a good first sentence!

That's expensive!!!

If you're going to be a network marketing professional, don't gamble. Simply test your headline or first sentence so you can be sure you have a winner.

Leverage? It is simple. Use headlines and first sentences that you know are winners.

Be a little outrageous.

Amazon Books is a great place to research and see if your topic or offer has merit. If the books on your topic are out of stock, or if they sell well, that means your topic is hot!

For instance, many years ago I ordered the book, *How to Make Your Man Behave in 21 Days or Less Using the Secrets of Professional Dog Trainers* - because I couldn't resist the great title. Just another example of how a great headline or first sentence sells. Hey, I hadn't even seen the book yet, but the title sold me.

My ultimate plan was to resell the book to my daughter at double the cover price. Unfortunately, I think she paid me with my credit card.

Guess what? The book quickly went out of stock. That told me relationship information was hot, but more importantly, that women desperately want to train men to respond to their verbal commands. (There is still a debate whether men have sufficient intelligence to be trainable ... but that's another story.)

I didn't have to go to Amazon to find out if that topic was hot. When I mentioned that I had purchased the book, almost all the women responded by saying, "Hey, could you loan me the book when your daughter is through with it?"

Years ago, Bawls Guarana energy drink had this message:

"So Powerful, You'll Need Coffee To Bring You Down. 10-Ounce Bottle Of Eye-Popping Refreshment."

Whoa! Now that gets attention.

So, wouldn't it be great if you had a product or service that had that kind of "pull through" appeal? Something where everyone wanted it just by hearing its name?

Well, you probably don't have a product or service with that kind of appeal. However, you could have a great first sentence or report that has that "pull through" appeal.

For example, maybe your first sentence, report or audio title could be:

* "All water is recycled ... our filter just takes out other people's contributions."

* "We call this the 'Nap Buster.'"

* "Does your boss laugh every time you ask for a raise?"

* "Instant weight-loss in a can."

* "Why middle managers die broke and depressed."

* "35 ice cream recipes for your diet."

* "Who said having a job is a good idea?"

* "Fat tablets, just for chocoholics."

* "My parents kicked me out of the house because I was making too much money."

* "How to make your teenagers adore you."

* "Avoid alarm clock stress and other work-related diseases."

* "What do your boss and three hyenas have in common?"

* "The skincare secret that will attract your future mate in less than 30 days."

* "Proof! This extra paycheck is legal."

* "Wipe out your car payments for life."

* "Get a full-time paycheck working a 12-hour week."

* "Slimmer thighs - fatter wallets."

* "The two best places to get unlimited promotions and pay raises."

* "Serum from the Fountain of Youth."

* "After two hip replacements, eye surgery and a kidney transplant, I thought now would be a good time to start taking care of my new body."

* "Work one time, get paid forever!"

* "Why health professionals recommend four cups of this coffee every day."

* "Golf 365 days a year while still banking your salary."

A little sensationalism never hurt to draw an audience.

More on headlines and first sentences.

I never get tired of great headlines and first sentences. Why? Because they are the deciding factors in whether our messages are effective or not.

You can't sell or recruit if no one is reading or hearing your message.

So here is a quick idea for creating a better headline.

Choose words that shock the reader into attention.

Your readers or listeners have many things going on inside their minds. Mortgage payments, job stress, family situations, etc. You will never be heard **unless** you can shock your readers or listeners out of their daydreams and into your presentation.

So, the next time you have to give a presentation, prepare yourself. Think of a great headline or first sentence that will get your prospect's immediate attention. It sure makes life easier.

How about a practical example for a product?

Let's use a product to illustrate how a good headline or first sentence would work by using interesting or shocking words. For this example I will use a "stop snoring spray" that we want to sell to our prospects.

First, we might decide to use a question as our headline or first sentence to get the prospects' attention.

Here are some ideas:

* "Are you sleeping with a freight train/jackhammer?" (They might say, "What are you talking about?" Then you would tell them that the average decibel range of a snore is the equivalent of a freight train or jackhammer.)

* "Do you suffer from Separate Bed Syndrome?"

* "Do you suffer from Bruised Rib Syndrome?"

* "Are you taking too many guest room vacations?"

* "Are you suffering from second-hand snoring?"

* "Do you need WD-40™ for the throat?"

* "Do you need rib protectors?"

All of these examples are designed to get your prospects to stop, think, and want more information. Now they will listen to your presentation.

But don't limit yourself to only thinking about a shocking verbal first sentence. How about creating a button, a slogan, or a headline for a small ad?

Want some examples?

* "Do you snore? Get relief now - ask me how."

* "Snoring relief - just a spray away."

* "Relief for second-hand snoring - ask me."

* "Snoring keeping you awake? Relief is just a spray away."

* "Silent sleep - spray the noise away."

* "Quiet sleep - quick relief."

* "Freight train keeping you up at night? Stop it in its tracks!"

* "Stop sleep abuse – the humane way."

* "Get a quiet night's sleep - give your partner the spray!"

* "Over 30 million men and women are victims - relief is just a spray away."

* "In America, 50% of the people snore and the other 50% have insomnia."

* "Sneak attack – spray a snorer."

Your choice of headlines and first sentences will make all the difference in the world. And if you don't make a good choice, here is what can happen!

You will be doomed to write titles for country/western songs!

Gasp! Nothing could be worse, right?

Want proof?

Here are some titles of country/western songs that did not go platinum or sell very well. See if you can pick up a trend.

* "If My Nose Were Full of Nickels, I'd Blow It All On You."

* "Mama Get The Hammer (There's a Fly On Papa's Head)."

* "May the Bird Of Paradise Fly Up Your Nose."

* "My Everyday Silver Is Plastic."

* "They May Put Me In Prison, But They Can't Stop My Face From Breakin' Out." (I can see an ad for an acne cure with this headline.)

* "I'm Just A Bug On The Windshield Of Life."

* "Velcro Arms, Teflon Heart."

* "I Got Tears In My Ears From Lying In My Bed On My Back Crying Over You."

* "You're The Reason Our Kids Are So Ugly."

* "Oh, I've Got Hair Oil On My Ears And My Glasses Are Slipping Down, But Baby I Can See Through You."

**Awwww, this is way too much fun.
How about a few more?**

* "You Can't Have Your Kate And Edith Too."

* "I've Been Flushed From The Bathroom Of Your Heart."

* "Her Teeth Were Stained, But Her Heart Was Pure."

* "Here's A Quarter, Call Someone Who Cares."

* "How Can I Miss You If You Won't Go Away?"

* "I Don't Know Whether To Kill Myself Or Go Bowling."

* "If The Phone Don't Ring, Baby, You'll Know It's Me."

* "If You Don't Leave Me Alone, I'll Go And Find Someone Else Who Will."

* "If You Leave Me, Can I Come Too?"

I am not making up these titles.

These are real titles of real country/western songs.

So spend some time developing great first sentences and headlines for every part of your business. This will make the biggest difference in how your prospects respond.

Enough humor, let's move on.

How to approach tough prospects, rejection-free.

On one of our annual MLM cruises, we shared tips every evening over the long, long dinners.

Richard Brooke, author of *Mach II with Your Hair on Fire*, shared this tip:

Most distributors will ask a tough prospect something like: "Would you take a look at this business opportunity and see if I should do it?"

This usually brings a negative review from the tough prospect.

Instead, ask the tough prospect this question: "Would you tell me how to become successful in my new business?"

What a great difference this question makes. You are more likely to get a positive response and interest by using this question.

And did you notice that there was only a small change of a few words?

Many distributors give up and say that network marketing doesn't work. Maybe they were only a few words away from success.

First Sentences for Network Marketing

Saying the wrong first sentence chases prospects away. Take the time to test new and better first sentences.

Cold-prospecting small business owners.

Simply walk into any small business on a main street and ask for the owner. When the owner extracts himself from the "crisis of the moment," casually say:

"I was just passing by. I didn't have a lot to do, so I thought I would stop by and interrupt your work. Now, I know you have a lot of things on your mind, cash flow problems, employee problems, tax form problems, landlord problems ... and you haven't seen your family in days ... but hey, let me tell you about **me**. Let me tell you about **my company**. Let me tell you about **my products and services**. Let me tell you about **my lifestyle**. Let me tell you about ... "

I wonder, is this how salesmen got their "warm and caring" reputation?

But you want to sponsor lots of small business owners, right? You know that they are entrepreneurs and hard workers, and that they take responsibility for their results. In other words, small business owners would be perfect for your business.

The only problem is ...

They don't want to talk to you.

Small business owners have their own lives, their own challenges, their own dreams, and very little time. You don't fit into their plans ... unless you become **part of their plans**.

Let's attack the first challenge now. Here is just one way to get time with small business owners.

The candy bar guilt trip.

About 25 years ago, I was listening to an audio by Rick Hill. Besides doing network marketing, Rick also sold radio advertising. He told the story of how he was able to get appointments with every small business in his area. It went something like this:

"Every day I would buy a couple boxes of candy bars. In the middle of the afternoon I would stop by small businesses. I knew the owners didn't have time for lunch and would be pretty hungry. I simply told the owner that I knew he was busy, didn't have time to eat lunch, gave him a candy bar, and then ... **left!**

"About a week later I would stop by the same small business owner and give him another candy bar.

"I would do this for three or four weeks. Finally, the small business owner would look forward to me stopping by. I had built some familiarity and trust.

"After those three or four weeks, the business owner, out of guilt and curiosity, would finally ask me what kind of business I was in. Now it was easy to talk to the business owner because he was asking me for a presentation."

Pretty simple, right?

This one little technique might be all you need to break into the small business market in your area.

Did you catch Rick's approach?

"I simply told the owner that I knew he was busy, didn't have time to eat lunch, gave him a candy bar, and then ... **left!**"

This separated Rick Hill from an ordinary bothersome salesman to someone the businessman would have an open-minded conversation with.

Now it is your turn to use a little creative thinking and common sense to apply this technique to your business.

For instance, you might notice that this technique would not be particularly effective with restaurants. I am sure the restaurant owner could find something to eat while he was busy.

Or, you might think:

"Wow! I sell nutritional cookies and nutritional food bars. I can have the small business owner experience the long-term energy of my product. Plus, I will be increasing my monthly volume of product moved and replacing that newspaper advertising budget."

* If you sold water filters, you could bring a container of nice, cold ice water.

* If you sold energy products, bring them by in the mid-afternoon when the owner's energy is at its lowest point.

* If you sold coffee, you could carry a thermos of hot water, some disposable coffee cups, and your gourmet coffee. Show up early!

First Sentences for Network Marketing

You get the idea. Just be creative.

Turning negatives into positive sales benefits.

Do you have a common complaint about your product, service or opportunity?

If you do, turn this negative into a positive. How?

A simple first sentence can solve that problem.

Want an example?

Let's say that your vitamin product costs twice as much as the competition. You could say this:

"You could get a weaker product for about half the price, but you don't want to be only half-healthy, do you?"

Or if the taste of your health drink is bad, you could say:

"When you taste our drink, you will **know** it is healthy and good for you, because you won't taste any sugar fillers that others use to dilute and weaken their drink."

Or if your skincare moisturizer is twice as expensive as your competition, you could say:

"You can have ordinary skin that eventually wrinkles and looks old, or you can use the best moisturizer in the world to keep your skin looking healthier and younger."

Or if your travel club charges more than the cheaper clubs, you could say:

"You don't want to be disappointed with a cheap holiday, as you have waited all year for your break from work. Make sure you will enjoy a proper holiday, not an aggravating one."

Or if your starting cost is $500 and your competition only charges $50, you could say:

"As you can see, this is a serious business that can help you earn a serious income, not some $50 gimmick that will leave you feeling cheated."

So take a look at your business now. Is there a negative that you have been trying to hide? Is there an objection that continues to hold prospects back from joining your business?

If you have a negative, don't worry. You can turn that negative into a great sales point with a great first sentence.

Just make a great offer!

Why not make a positive offer in your opening question or statement?

By telling your prospect your offer, you naturally select those prospects who say, "Hey! That sounds great!" Our offers will **create** pre-sold prospects.

Some product and services examples:

"Save 20 cents a gallon at the gas pump!"

"How to earn a bonus check every time your neighbor picks up his telephone."

"For hemorrhoid sufferers: You'll never have to say 'Ouch' again."

"Never crave another cigarette again."

"How to make your grandchildren the smartest children in their neighborhood."

A few diet product examples:

"This is the secret ingredient that weight-loss doctors personally use to lose weight."

"Magic food helps burn unwanted body fat while you drive to work."

"Let our herbal fat-burner help you lose weight while you watch television."

"Four secrets thin people never tell you."

"21 foods that accelerate weight loss."

"Let our protein shake slim your body while you watch soap operas."

Some health & wellness examples:

"31-year-old skydiver discovers the secret to soft, moist, younger skin."

"Four reasons to take our secret vitamin supplement every day."

"How to have more energy than your hyperactive three-year-old."

"How to have mountain fresh air for a good night's sleep."

Lots of opportunity examples:

"Get three paychecks a month instead of two."

"How a secretary from Central City shows people how to fire their boss."

"Exactly why you should fire your dream-sucking, vampire boss now."

"How two high school students doubled their college funds by helping neighbors save on long-distance phone charges."

"How a housewife from Russell earned $3,121 in only 12 days."

"9 great reasons to quit your job now."

"47-year-old office worker starts work on Monday morning with a smile."

"21-year-old housewife earns more money part-time than her overworked husband does full-time."

"Overworked government employee shows ordinary taxpayers how to save an additional $1,590 a year."

"How to get everything in life that you want ... but don't deserve."

Carlos to the rescue.

My friend, Carlos, figured out that printing single-sided cards with only the offer brought the cost down to just pennies per card. He left the cards wherever a prospect might pick one up - telephone booths, hotel lobbies, with cab drivers, you name it! Once again, his phone began to ring with people actively looking to make extra money - in other words, hot prospects!

You have already guessed what happened next. Leaders in his downline realized that no matter how small their marketing budget, they could afford to put business cards anywhere potential prospects might run across them. Prospecting became affordable and rejection-free! Everyone could do this ... if the offer got prospects to call.

Yes, it is all about having a good offer.

Now, you don't have to print single-sided cards with your offer. You could put your offer on the back of your current business card also. No problem.

Make your own offer.

Remember, you are not limited to any one offer. You can make an offer for a product or service that you offer through your network marketing business. Here are a few examples of offers other distributors have on their cards. Now, all of these offers follow a little formula. You will learn about this formula in an upcoming chapter. But for now, enjoy.

* "How a 48-year-old architect from Queens, NY stopped snoring in just 3 seconds, after keeping his wife awake for 21 years! For details, call 123-456-7890."

* "How a 31-year-old, overworked nanny from Houston, TX shows people how to get 3 hours of extra energy every day, without drugs! For details, call 123-456-7890."

* "How a 26-year-old social worker from Redlands, CA shows people how to get unlimited access to top-quality attorneys for less than 83 cents per day! For details, call 123-456-7890."

* "How a mother from Atlanta, GA with two children helped a 332-pound woman fit into a size 6 bikini in just 5 months! For details, call 123-456-7890."

* "How a near-sighted airline captain from Columbus, OH shows people how to exchange their jobs for more free time in just 9 months. For details, call 123-456-7890."

This method of creating prospects may or may not be for you, but I suggest you let everyone in your downline know about it. You will have distributors take this idea straight to the bank, and that makes good business sense for everyone!

Bad and confusing first sentences and headlines.

"It's not what you say, but what your prospects understand that counts."

I believe that headlines and first sentences are almost everything. If you don't capture the prospect's attention instantly, he will never listen to your beautiful presentation.

Most presentations assume that you have a motivated, interested, focused, and polite prospect sitting in front of you just hanging on to your every word. Ha ha ha. When was the last time that ever happened to you?

I plead with networkers to seriously **test** and **review** their headlines and first sentences. If these openings are bad, well, you are sabotaging your entire presentation. You are "roadkill" before you even start.

Why start your presentations with a handicap?

Instead, try to be clear so that you have the best chance for success.

If you don't think this is a problem, look at the media. These highly-trained professionals have written the following headlines that can easily be misunderstood. Yes, these are real headlines that went bad:

* "Something Went Wrong in Jet Crash, Expert Says."

First Sentences for Network Marketing

* "Plane Too Close to Ground, Crash Probe Told."

* "Police Begin Campaign to Run Down Jaywalkers."

* "Safety Experts Say School Bus Passengers Should Be Belted."

* "Two Sisters Reunited After 18 Years in Checkout Counter."

* "House Passes Gas Tax Onto Senate."

* "Drunk Gets Nine Months In Violin Case."

* "Kids Make Nutritious Snacks."

* "NJ Judge To Rule On Nude Beach."

* "Eye Drops Off Shelf."

* "Squad Helps Dog Bite Victim."

* "If Strike Isn't Settled Quickly It May Last A While."

* "Enraged Cow Injures Farmer With Ax."

* "Blind Woman Gets New Kidney From Dad She Hasn't Seen In Years."

* "Two Soviet Ships Collide - One Dies."

* "Enfield Couple Slain; Police Suspect Homicide."

* "Miners Refuse to Work After Death."

* "Include Your Children When Baking Cookies."

* "Motorcycle For Sale: Will Trade For Wheelchair."

* "MLM Vitamin Distributorship For Sale Due To Poor Health."

First Sentences for Network Marketing

* "Third Annual Going Out Of Business Sale."

* "Divorce Sale: His Stuff Cheap."

These confusing headlines aren't limited to newspapers. Here are some signs that could use a bit of headline and first sentence editing:

In the window of an Oregon store: "Why go elsewhere and be cheated when you can come here?"

On a Tennessee highway: "When this sign is under water, this road is impassable."

In a Maine restaurant: "Open 7 days a week and weekends."

At a Santa Fe gas station: "We will not sell gasoline to anyone in a glass container."

In a Florida maternity ward: "No children allowed."

In a Tacoma, Washington men's clothing store: "15 men's wool suits, $10. They won't last an hour!"

A long-established dry cleaner's sign: "38 years on the same spot."

A local grocery store: "Stock up and save! Limit 1 per customer."

In the window of a Kentucky appliance store: "Don't kill your wife. Let our washing machine do the dirty work."

In a clothing store: "Wonderful bargains for men with 16 and 17 necks."

In a funeral parlor: "Ask about our layaway plan."

Okay, just one more bit of humor.

And while on the subject of confusing headlines and first sentences, here is my favorite cute headline from a Salem, Massachusetts newspaper:

"Midget Fortune Teller Escapes From Jail; Police Look For Small Medium At Large."

Yes, that is a cute headline, but it takes a while to understand it. Most prospects won't take the effort to decode your cute headline.

So stick with clear, benefit-laden headlines. Don't make your prospects work too hard.

Enough smiling. Let's get serious.

The easiest way to be understandable is by making a clear offer. Want some examples?

* "Legal advice and assistance by telephone for only $25 a month."

* "How to wake up every morning feeling like a million dollars!"

* "Make your skin look 20 years younger in only 45 seconds a day."

* "How to work three weeks out of every month, but get paid for four."

* "Sell your alarm clock to your neighbor."

* "Take five-star holidays for the price of a Holiday Inn."

* "Stop your skin from wrinkling while you sleep."

* "Daycare is not a substitute for good parenting."

* "Build a full-time income in six months, without leaving your job."

Just remember this. If your prospect is confused, or can't clearly understand your first sentence or headline, that is just as bad as having a terrible first sentence or headline. You won't connect with your prospect.

Can't think of a good first sentence or headline?

Do you have trouble thinking of a great first sentence that will get your prospects to open their minds and get excited?

Here is the easiest way to get great first sentence and headline ideas.

Model the professionals.

Magazines, tabloids, and cheap trashy newspapers have only one thing they can sell the potential reader: **headlines**. When you are at a newsstand, you don't have time to read the articles. You only have time to skim over the headlines as you make a decision on which newspaper or magazine to buy.

Most publications hire expensive professional copywriters to create interesting headlines. Why not use their creativity to get your imagination started? You can read their expensive headlines and modify them to fit your network marketing business.

For instance, on a past MLM cruise, two of the Slovenian network marketing distributors noticed a magazine on a newsstand in the Virgin Islands. The magazine was called *Woman's Own*. This publication filled their entire front cover with headlines because **headlines sell.**

Let's take some of these headlines and **modify** them for our network marketing business. Remember, we can use these headlines for first sentences in our personal and group presentations also. Better first sentences will make our meetings and presentations more exciting for our prospects.

Women's Own **headline:** "Lose 7 Pounds in Three Days! Flush The Fat Out."

Our headline: "Save $1,500 Yearly! Small Business Tax Deductions Available To Anyone!

Women's Own **headline:** "Loving A Man Who's Cheated. Marriages Can Survive an Affair, Here's How."

Our headline: "Broke After Surviving 20 Years Of Job Slavery? How To Build A Massive Savings Account With Your Own Part-Time Business."

Women's Own **headline:** "The One Flaw That Makes A Man An Impossible Mate."

Our headline: "The One Flaw That Will Destroy Your Career Every Time."

Women's Own **headline:** "Big Decision? Meet Three Psychics Who Can Help."

Our headline: "Unsure About Your Financial Future? Meet Three Entrepreneurs Who Will Change Your Life Forever."

Women's Own **headline:** "There Are Ways To Find A Life Partner: 10 Secrets From The World's Leading Matchmakers."

Our headline: "You Can Retire In Five Years: 10 Secrets From Local Networking Entrepreneurs."

As you can see, this "Create A Similar Headline Game" is easy. The more you do it, the better your headlines and first sentences become. Try practicing this technique everywhere you go. When you see a great headline on a billboard or advertisement, convert the headline to a powerful network marketing headline.

This isn't the only way to create great headlines and first sentences. It just happens to be a quick and easy way that works.

Even computer magazines have good headlines.

Women's magazines are the best, but there are even good copy ideas in computer magazines. Let's try modeling one now.

"The Amazonian piranha uses razor-sharp teeth to **rip out bloody chunks** of your **quivering** flesh until you **thrash** and **convulse** in **mind-numbing agony** and **plead** for someone to **kill you**. (Sort of like using someone else's network fax solution.)"

Notice how the author used verbs. Verbs make the headline strong. Too many amateur headline writers grab the nearest thesaurus and try to make the headline interesting by using fancy adjectives. Adjectives are weak. Verbs are strong.

If you think the headline is too long, that's okay. It doesn't matter what we think. **It is what the prospect thinks that counts.** Research shows that **longer headlines pull better** than shorter headlines.

So here is our version for network marketing:

"The I.R.S. uses its **blood-sucking** deductions to **shrivel** your paycheck so that you slave away in work **bondage** until you are 65 ... then you can **starve to death** on 40% of your original income."

Too gruesome? Maybe. However, it will make people wince. The headline is emotional and causes people to think.

Remember, this headline doesn't have to be in print. It could be one of the first phrases out of your mouth during a recruiting presentation. Or, maybe you can open your opportunity meeting with this first sentence.

The results from using better headlines? Well, try opening next week's opportunity meeting with a powerful first sentence. Then, watch the prospects lean forward and open their minds. Get ready for an explosion in your networking business.

Your "Ice Breaker" first sentence.

When you change the subject from personal issues to your business, you will need a great sentence to capture your prospect's interest.

Sure, you can start a conversation by saying **useless** things such as these popular phrases:

1. "Hi, how are you?"

2. "Great weather today."

3. "Where are you from?"

4. "Nice jacket."

5. "How are the wife and kids?"

6. "What's new?"

7. "How about that basketball game last night?"

These first sentences are useless. We are not introducing our business to prospects. We are engaging in idle "chit-chat" instead of letting our prospect know what we're offering.

Just compare the opening sentences in these two examples.

Example A: "Yeah, nice talking to you, and by the way, have you considered that your income options are limited by your linear-income job?" (Groan.)

Example B: "Yeah, nice talking to you, and I am just curious, would you like to travel more if someone else paid for it?"

Hmmm. Which example might get the better response? It is obvious. A well-thought-out first sentence is important, especially as an "Ice Breaker." For "Ice Breaker" first sentences, I wrote a whole book of formulas for "Ice Breakers" available at http://www.BigAlBooks.com.

A bad transition from social chit-chat to introducing your business could be deadly. And if your distributors don't have great first sentences to introduce their business into the conversation, they won't say anything because they fear rejection.

You must find a comfortable way to tell prospects what you do. If your prospects are interested, they will ask for more information.

You don't have to sell them.

You don't have to ask for the order.

You don't have to ask them a leading question that puts them in an uncomfortable corner.

If you try to sell prospects or make them uncomfortable, you force your prospects to think of ways to reject you. They want to avoid a presentation so they say things like this:

* "I'm not interested."

* "Oh, that's a pyramid."

* "I am too busy."

* "My friend used to do that and it didn't work."

* "Somebody in China lost money once."

* "I am allergic to everything."

* "I'm only 44 years away from retirement."

* "Oh, that is too expensive."

* "I would never do something like that."

Old people in the Ukraine.

Here is another example of the importance of choosing the right sentence. You might remember it from my book about stories.

I was in the Ukraine talking to about 400 old people. I knew they were old because I was the youngest person there. I asked them, "So what did you say to keep all the young people away?"

Well, they didn't have a sense of humor about that question. They insisted young people weren't interested in their products or opportunity. Finally, I asked them, "Well, if you meet someone who is 18 years old, what is your first sentence?"

They replied, "You can retire five years early with our great opportunity!"

Ouch.

Five years early is about 40 years away for an 18-year-old. Not very motivating. No wonder no young people were in attendance.

When you meet an 18-year-old prospect, what could you say that would be a better first sentence? How about:

* "Would it be okay if you didn't have to work 40 years like your parents?"

* "Would you like to travel more and still get paid?"

* "I just found out how we can choose our own hours when we work."

* "Do you want to spend your life as an employee?"

* "How do you feel about waking up at 7am and commuting to a job every day?"

* "Do you get enough holidays to do the traveling on your wish list?"

* "Does your job interfere with your week?"

* "Would you like to earn more money part-time than your professor does full-time?"

Not your style?

Maybe you like a safer, more subtle approach. Or maybe you want an "Ice Breaker" technique that only locates people who **want** to do your business. The above are only sample suggestions.

That's why skills are important. If you have skills, you will have many proven "Ice Breakers" to choose from.

If you don't have skills ... well, it is going to be hard.

I don't care how excited you are, how positive you are, and how many goals you set. Eventually you'll have to **say something or do something**.

And that is where skills come into your success.

To kickstart your imagination.

* "Are you in deep money-trouble? Excellent, let's talk."

* "Are you in shape ... financially?"

* "Are you in the rat race and the rats are winning?"

* "Are you losing sleep from stress?"

* "Are you making all the money you need?"

* "Are you NEXT?"

* "Are you overworked and underpaid?"

* "Are you planning to retire before you die?"

* "Are your dreams worth going for?"

* "Are you a know-it-all? Get the last word on making money!"

* "Are you career-frustrated?"

* "Are you flushing your money down the toilet?"

Your signature file at the end of your emails.

Here is a great place to attract prospects to your business or product with no rejection. By choosing the right first sentence for your signature file, you can get people to take action and ask for a presentation.

If you are not familiar with a signature file, it is the "P.S." at the end of your email message.

You must make your signature file interesting so that your prospects will have a reason to visit your website or call you. Here is a signature file I successfully used to add over 2,000 subscribers to my newsletter.

P.S. Are men better networkers than women? Here's proof:

http://LINK

I also used:

P.S. For a laugh and to see my wife's face, click here:

http://LINK

Both signature file links sent people to a short 15-second video presentation. The video presentation was created by my 15-year-old nephew.

Cost? A six-pack of beer. (Just kidding. His mom wouldn't let me.) So, I took him to Starbucks to get hyper-caffeinated as a reward for his one hour of programming.

The signature files worked well because:

P.S. Are men better networkers than women? Here's proof:

http://LINK

and

P.S. For a laugh and to see my wife's face, click here:

http://LINK

created **tension** and **curiosity**. If your teaser lines and first sentences are boring, they just won't work.

Because the video presentation was funny, people passed on the link to their co-workers and friends. The viral effect was massive.

At the end of the video presentation was an offer for 77 FREE Tips. About 45% of the viewers subscribed. Now I had 77 **more** chances to create a relationship with the prospect.

This technique was one of the least expensive, yet most effective ways for me to create qualified prospects.

So what could you use for your signature files? Here are several examples to get you thinking:

* Click here to see which picture looks like you.

* Does this look like your annual holiday? Click here.

* Click here to see a picture of my boss' face when I told him, "I quit."

* Does your telephone bill look like this? Click here to see a picture of my bill.

* Click here to see my mother's "before" and "after" pictures.

* Click here to see a 7-second movie of my daily commute.

* Click here to see a picture of my wife's stomach.

* Click here to see how a 46-year-old grandmother gets free travel tickets to visit her grandchildren.

* Click here to see a picture of the free car I chose. You won't believe what I picked.

* Here is a picture of a strange "bonus" check I received in the mail yesterday.

* Want a four-day work week? Click here to see how.

What do all these examples have in common?

They are interesting. They create curiosity. And these examples direct readers to your website.

Did you notice that most of these signature files started with a call to action? "Click here to see a picture of" is a great motivator that directs prospects to take action.

So what does a boring signature file look like?

Like this:

119

"The world's best home-based incredible business opportunity with lifestyle enhancement features. Voted #1 by somebody. Go to:

http://www.mytotallyboringopportunitypage.com/1234/id=j2kt4/lostinspace"

Now that is bad.

So if you don't have a signature file now, it costs nothing to add to your emails. Just make sure it is good.

A headline for your ad.

There are books upon books on headlines.

If the headline doesn't grab the readers' attention, no one will read what comes next. That means no matter how good your opportunity, your products, your services or your offer ... no one will **see** what you have unless you capture their attention first with your headline.

Headlines are the most important part of your ad. Want proof?

Remember our earlier example? Do you read every article in your daily newspaper? Of course not. So how do you choose which articles to read?

By the headlines.

For instance, let's see what you do as you skim your paper and see the following headlines:

"Conflict continues in Europe." (Same headline every day, I think I'll move on and read another article.)

"Fire destroys lots of buildings." (Okay. That's terrible, but this does happen a lot.)

"Government proposes to pass more laws." (Nothing unusual here.)

"Elvis Presley's two-headed great-grandchild elopes with two-headed alien." (Hmmm, I'd better read this article.)

What's happening?

Why did we choose to read only the last article?

Because it was **interesting**. Our lives are busy and we don't want to waste time reading boring articles. We want a little excitement.

And tabloids know this.

Check out all those cheap, trashy, sleazy tabloids at the checkout counter in your local supermarket or newsstand. What do they really have to sell?

A great sports section? No.

Outstanding investigative journalism? No.

In-depth business reports? No.

Interesting headlines? Yes.

That's all they have to sell – just headlines. And they do an excellent job of selling their tabloids because we love their interesting headlines.

What are some examples of interesting, tabloid-like headlines that you could use for your ads? Here are a few of my favorites that entice the reader to read further:

* "Atlanta Housewife Investigated and Almost Arrested For Losing 73 Pounds."

* "Overweight Granny Loses 57 Pounds, Steals Granddaughter's Tight-Fitting Jeans, Then Enters Limbo Contest."

If you wanted to lose weight, you would definitely choose to read the rest of these ads. Why? Because the headlines are interesting.

So what makes certain headlines interesting?

Well, when we talk about people, it's interesting. That is why soap operas get such high ratings. That is why picture-filled gossip magazines have so many readers. We like to peek into other people's lives.

And adding specifics to your headlines makes them more believable, too. That's why I include specific odd numbers in my five-step formula.

Are you ready for the five-step formula so that you can create cheap, sleazy, trashy (but very interesting) tabloid-like headlines? Here it is:

Step #1: Benefit

Step #2: Occupation

Step #3: Geography

Step #4: Odd numbers

Step #5: Personality

That's it! This special "Big Al" five-step formula for interesting tabloid headlines will help you create great first sentences that will capture your prospects' attention. Use these headlines or first sentences, and they will create the interest you are looking for in your prospects.

It looks simple, but let's put it to use to give us some interesting headlines.

Step 1: Let's pick a benefit for our product.

Imagine that we sell tax advice to entrepreneurs. Our headline should include a benefit (saving taxes), so our headline would say:

"How to save money on your taxes."

Good start, but it could be better. Let's go on to:

Step #2: Occupation.

Maybe the tax advisor used to be a bank teller. Now we can improve our headline to say:

"Underpaid bank teller shows ordinary people how to save money on their taxes."

Better headline, isn't it? There is more interest with this revision. But we can do more.

Let's go on to:

Step #3. Geography.

Maybe our tax advisor lives in Weird Falls, Virginia. Now we can improve our headline more by saying:

"Underpaid bank teller from Weird Falls, Virginia shows ordinary people how to save money on their taxes."

Specifying a geographic location adds a credibility factor to our prospect. If you wanted to save money on your taxes, you would read this ad, wouldn't you?

We have two more steps to go:

Step #4: Odd numbers.

Now which has more credibility?

1. "About a thousand."

2. "973."

When we say "973" to someone, it is more believable because it is **specific**. So now we add some odd numbers to our headline to get:

"Underpaid bank teller from Weird Falls, Virginia shows ordinary people how to save $751 on their tax return by adding just one little form."

You definitely want to read this ad now to find out which form to add to your tax return.

And finally:

Step #5: Personality.

People love personality. That is why we read Hollywood gossip, watch movies and television shows. Boring people become lecturers. People with personalities become entertainers.

By adding a word or two of personality, we make this first sentence come alive.

What kind of words describe personality? How about:

* Boring

* Energetic

* Honest

* Semi-honest

* Loving

* Caring

* Hyperactive

* Overbearing

* Often-sober

* Creative

* Courageous

* Cowardly

* Shy

* Outgoing

Those are just a start. Let's add some personality as step #5, and our first sentence becomes:

"Boring, underpaid bank teller from Weird Falls, Virginia shows ordinary people how to save $751 on their tax return by adding just one little form."

So how could we use this sentence?

Let's say that you are about to give your one-minute speech at a networking event. You could start off your speech by saying:

"Let me tell you how a boring, underpaid bank teller from Weird Falls, Virginia shows ordinary people how to save $751 on their tax return by adding just one little form."

You now have the full attention of the audience. Just that easy.

Want some more examples using this simple five-step formula?

Step #1 (benefit):

"How to stop snoring."

Step #2 (occupation):

"How a car mechanic accidentally discovered how to stop snoring."

Step #3 (geography):

"How a car mechanic from Wabonsie Center shows people how to stop snoring."

Step #4 (odd numbers):

"61-year-old car mechanic from Wabonsie Center discovers how to stop snoring in only 13 seconds."

Step #5 (personality):

"How a greasy 61-year-old car mechanic from Wabonsie Center discovered how to stop snoring in only 13 seconds."

Want to do it again?

Step #1 (benefit):

"How to make more money."

Step #2 (occupation):

"Beautician's assistant shows mothers how to make more money."

Step #3 (geography):

"Beautician's assistant from Diamond County shows mothers how to make more money."

Step #4 (odd numbers):

"21-year-old beautician's assistant from Diamond County shows mothers how to earn an extra $323 a month."

Step #5 (personality):

"21-year-old beautician's assistant from Diamond County shows overworked and stressed mothers how to earn an extra $323 a month."

One more time?

Step #1 (benefit):

"How to work from home."

Step #2 (occupation):

"Former waitress shows people how to work from home."

Step #3 (geography):

"Former New York City waitress shows people how to work from home."

Step #4 (odd numbers):

"31-year old former New York City waitress shows people how to work from home."

Step #5 (personality):

"Introverted 31-year old former New York City waitress shows people how to work from home."

Is this the only way to make interesting headlines and first sentences?

No. It is just an easy, five-step formula to get you started. Once you have your "Big Al" cheap, sleazy, trashy, five-step tabloid-like headline or first sentence, you can edit and fine-tune the sentence to fit your needs.

The subject line of your emails.

How easy is it to delete an email?

People quickly judge their emails by:

#1. Who sent the email.

#2. The subject line of the email.

Your subject line is a filter to your readers.

If your reader doesn't recognize your email address, he then goes to the subject line to see if the message is spam.

Avoid subject lines that appear to be selling something. Make your subject line as personal as possible. Your message is only a click or two away from deletion, so make your subject line interesting.

It should be obvious, but avoid words in the subject line such as:

* Viagra.

* Opportunity.

* Earn.

* Sex.

* SpyCam.

* Free. (Yes, this could be a turn-off. Test it.)

* Insurance.

* Discount, etc.

Next, see which words and phrases turn off prospects.

Some words turn off prospects while other words make your offer stand out from the crowd. This is important if your email is competing against 100 other emails the prospect receives that day.

So do you know which words **motivate** prospects?

How do you know which words instantly **shut down** your prospect's desire to investigate your program further?

It is easy to know. Just put yourself in your prospects' shoes. Here is how I do it.

First, I make sure I don't turn off the prospects' motivation with old, tired phrases that say, "This is just another one of those network marketing schemes."

Second, I try to avoid the over-exaggeration that destroys credibility.

Third, I cheat. I read my email and look at the subject lines.

I just read other people's subject lines and learn **what not to say**. Yes, what not to say.

After reading 50 or 60 bad subject lines trying to entice someone to open their email and join a new company, suddenly the offers start looking alike. The offers become a blur. You glance at the subject line, delete the email, and repeat.

Here is what I mean. These are the actual subject lines of offers I have seen ... and my thoughts.

* **Show Me The Money! 20 x 20 = $100,000+** (Oh yeah, this sounds credible.)

* **Go From $0 To Over $200,000 In Just 60 days! I Can Prove It!** (I guess the proof was in the attachment that didn't come through.)

* **The World's First Complete System For Creating Wealth!** (Haven't I heard this somewhere before? Yeah, yesterday two other offers claimed to be the first, best, and most complete system.)

* **The Winning Team Success System (TM). The Most Successful Sponsoring System In The World!** (Is this better than The World's First Complete System?)

* **The New "In" Tea, The Hottest MLM Lead Program In The Industry! 2 x 10 Global Force Spillover Matrix. No Sponsoring Required!** (Is this better than the previous program? If no sponsoring is required, then where does the spillover come from?)

* **An Awesome Money-Making System. No-Brainer Social Media Program - No Personal Contact.** (Maybe they should personally contact the previous two emailers and compare systems?)

* **The Gold Lead Pool. Forced Overflow Expanding Matrix! Recruiting NOT Required - But Handsomely Rewarded!** (No work. No recruiting. I wonder if I even have to fill out an application.)

* **1-Year-Old Solid Debt-Free Company. New Improved Compensation Plan!** (I guess they are debt-free because their background is so bad, they can't qualify for

credit. Glad to hear about their new and improved compensation plan. The old plan must have been awful.)

* **If You Didn't Make $20,000 Last Month, Read This!** (And then the email tells me I will only earn 5-8 thousand a week for the first few weeks. Bummer!)

* **Timing Is Everything! No Binary! No 1/3 Rule! No Mailouts! No Phone Calls! No Monthly Payments!** (No bonus check either?)

* **I Will Build Your Business For You! I Will Work For You For FREE.** (Sure, and will you pay me a salary while I watch you work?)

Certainly some of these words and phrases are motivating by themselves, but after your prospects have been bombarded with these offers, you don't want to sound like all the other offers.

Here's a partial list of "red flag" phrases that warn prospects to watch out for the catch:

* Everyone earns money with this plan.

* Earn $xxx in the next seven days.

* Stop wasting your time with other programs.

* The hottest new program of the century.

* Pre-launch, pre-enrollment, pre-ground-floor.

* I am only two generations down from a heavy hitter.

* No work, no sponsoring, no retailing.

* The only system, the best system, the revolutionary system, the system to end all systems.

* Once-in-a-lifetime opportunity.

* Be first. Join before your downline joins.

* The perfect opportunity.

* Get in now, before it is too late.

* We build your downline for you.

* Call now so that I can place you at the top.

* No meetings. No paperwork. No products.

* Awesome money-making program.

I'm sure you can add to this list.

These phrases yell **"Warning! Warning!"** to our prospects. I try to avoid these phrases and words in my headlines and presentations.

Well, if we are trying to avoid all these phrases, then what do we say? What kind of words and phrases can we use to attract prospects and give our opportunity credibility?

The first sentence your reader sees in your email is your subject line. A little curiosity can motivate your reader to open your email and continue.

Some examples?

I just looked in my spam folder and here are some of the better subject lines:

* Smoking Cessation: Learn How To Live Cigarette-Free.

* Exciting New CARB-BLOCKER Is All The Rage In Hollywood!

* Facelift In A Bottle!

* Do This To Reverse Your Diabetes.

* Federal Rebates Pay for Solar.

* Long-Suppressed SECRET To Normalized Blood Sugar.

* You Could Be Feeding This 'Dangerous Food' To Your Family.

* Try Before You Buy - Lower Your Blood Sugar.

* Take A Fairytale Vacation To Ireland.

* What Your Power Company Doesn't Want You To Know.

You want your subject line to filter and sort interested prospects for you, but you don't want your subject line to reveal too much. If you say everything in your subject line, there is no motivation to open your email and read your story or offer.

Here are some examples of the subject line telling everything, and risking that the prospect will make a final decision based upon the few characters in the subject line:

* How About HD Free For 24 months - Learn More About The Best DISH Ever!

* Protect And Beautify Your Garage Floor.

* The World's Leading Dating Service.

* Rates Going Lower? Qualify For Government HARP Program Today.

* Clinically Proven Anti-Aging Supplement Is Here.

* Protective Coating For Concrete, Steel And Wood - 35% off.

* Claim Your CVS Coupon.

* Can You Qualify For An FHA Refinance?

You can learn a lot just by reading the subject lines in your spam folder. :)

But how about your business?

Let's create some curiosity and interest with some custom subject lines now.

* How my mother lost weight without dieting.

* This is how my daughter finally got rid of her teenage acne.

* Never worry about your electric bill again. Here is how ...

* Where to take your family vacation ... and save money.

* Tell this to your boss on Monday morning and see ...

* Why smart people have an extra paycheck.

* Create a part-time check that pays for your mortgage.

* Sleep in until the crack of noon. Forget commuting.

* Don't die on your job. How to quit early.

* Jobs interfere with the week. How to cut back.

* How to get your business to make your car payments for you.

Our emails are worthless if no one reads them. A little common sense like these tips can make us more effective.

The subject line of your social network postings.

While on a three-week cruise, I got bored. There was a lot of ocean on our way past Antarctica, so I decided to pass the time looking at forums and social media.

Since it was late December, I posted a lesson on setting and achieving goals on a forum for network marketers. Seemed appropriate.

Here was the subject line of my post that appeared to readers of the forum:

Slipped by me like a "Vaseline-coated ninja."

Remember this first sentence.

Now, when the readers clicked on my post, they saw the rest of my post. I talked about how the year went by quickly, how I didn't achieve the goals I wanted, and how I came up with a 13-page solution to that problem that they could download at no charge.

Let's review. No one will see my post with my free download offer **unless** they click on the first sentence in the subject line of the post.

So is that sentence important? Yes!

Does the first sentence make a difference?

Absolutely. Here is proof.

Immediately after the subject line, this forum showed how many times each message was read.

Here are the view totals for a few of the messages before my post, and a few after. Look closely at the view numbers:

* Giving it time is the key (views: 13)

* Hello - I am new to this forum (views: 63)

* Hi Jason...I am old to this forum! (views: 23)

* Re: Welcome to the Family! (views: 14)

* MLM -vs- CDM (views: 74)

* Slipped by me like a "Vaseline-coated ninja" ... (views: 134)

* Wow!... (views: 78)

* Deregulation Industry (views: 74)

* Saturday Profile (views: 64)

* Can you read? (views: 70)

* Try A Chat Room (views: 56)

The least interesting first sentence got only 13 people to read further.

The most interesting first sentence, "Slipped by me like a 'Vaseline-coated ninja'" received **ten times** as many people to read further!

Think about this.

By just changing the first sentence, our efforts went ten times further. That is a great way to leverage your time. Don't you think it might be wise to invest a few more minutes making that first sentence more attractive?

Or, imagine we had to pay for this post. If we had a good first sentence, maybe that post would get us all the business we needed. And if our first sentence was bad, we would have to pay for 10 posts, ten times as much, to get the same number of leads.

So what else could we say?

Okay, makes sense to have better first sentences and headlines in social media. How about a few ideas to get your imagination going:

* "Secret breakfast food helps burn body fat while you drive to work."

* "69-year-old grandmother changes her diet, becomes arthritis-free, and begins teaching karate."

* "9 great reasons to quit your job now."

* "Three questions you should ask your boss tomorrow."

* "How to extend that two-week vacation."

* "Three quick shortcuts for busy mothers."

* "Free booklet shows you how to keep your children healthy."

* "Increase your take-home pay by $450!"

* "Willpower in a bottle."

* "How to change the size of your paycheck."

* "Here is a picture of me at 9am in the morning."

* "Take ten coffee breaks a day ... and get paid for it."

* "Here is how I get paid to travel."

* "How to have a five-day weekend instead of a two-day weekend."

And the rest is up to you!

You will see examples of great first sentences everywhere! Just observe. Once we know that first sentences are the key, we are on a lifelong quest to improve them.

Remember, some prospects will say, "I am not interested."

But, they may not be turning down our product, service, or opportunity ... they may just be turning down how we describe it.

Our job is to stop blaming uninterested prospects.

Our job is to be more interesting.

FREE!

Get 7 mini-reports of amazing, easy sentences that create new, hot prospects.

Discover how just a few correct words can change your network marketing results forever.

Get all seven free Big Al mini-reports, and the free weekly Big Al Report with more recruiting and prospecting tips.

Sign up today at:

http://www.BigAlReport.com

MORE BIG AL RESOURCES

Want Big Al to speak in your area?

Request a Big Al training event:

http://www.BigAlSeminars.com

MORE BOOKS BY
TOM "BIG AL" SCHREITER

The Four Color Personalities for MLM
The Secret Language for Network Marketers

Ice Breakers!
How To Get Any Prospect To Beg You For A Presentation

How To Get Instant Trust, Belief, Influence and Rapport!
13 Ways To Create Open Minds By Talking To The
Subconscious Mind

Big Al's MLM Sponsoring Magic
How to Build a Network Marketing Team Quickly

How To Prospect, Sell And Build Your Network Marketing
Business With Stories

26 Instant Marketing Ideas To Build Your Network
Marketing Business

How To Build Network Marketing Leaders Volume One:
Step-By-Step Creation Of MLM Professionals

How To Build Network Marketing Leaders Volume Two:
Activities And Lessons For MLM Leaders

Start SuperNetworking! 5 Simple Steps To Creating Your
Own Personal Networking Group

Complete list at:

http://www.BigAlBooks.com

See a full line of Big Al products at:

http://www.FortuneNow.com

ABOUT THE AUTHOR

Tom "Big Al" Schreiter has 40+ years of experience in network marketing and MLM. As the author of the original "Big Al" training books in the late '70s, he has continued to speak in over 80 countries on using the exact words and phrases to get prospects to open up their minds and say "YES."

His passion is marketing ideas, marketing campaigns, and how to speak to the subconscious mind in simplified, practical ways. He is always looking for case studies of incredible marketing campaigns that give usable lessons.

As the author of numerous audio trainings, Tom is a favorite speaker at company conventions and regional events.

His blog, **http://www.BigAlBlog.com** is a regular update of network marketing and MLM business-building ideas.

Anyone can subscribe to his free weekly tips at:

http://www.BigAlReport.com

53095410R00082

Made in the USA
Lexington, KY
21 June 2016